Alternative Education

(*Strictly on the basis of prescribed syllabus with modern trends*)

Alternative Education

(Strictly on the basis of prescribed syllabus with modern trends)

Tushar K Sinha

AUTHORSPRESS

Worldwide Circulation through Authorspress Global Network
First Published 2008
by
Authorspress
E-35/103, Jawahar Park
Laxmi Nagar, Delhi-110 092
e-mail: authorspress@yahoo.com

Alternative Education
ISBN 978-81-7273-465-7

Printed in India at Tarun Offset, Delhi.

Preface

Throughout history societies have sought to educate their people to produce goods and services, to respond effectively and creatively to their world, and to satisfy their curiosity and aesthetic impulses. To achieve any of these objectives people need to acquire reliable knowledge and to think systematically, for which formal schools, keeping abreast of the latest developments in various fields of knowledge, are established by governments and private agencies worldwide. Nonetheless, the evolving economic, political and social needs of society, in conjunction with differing philosophies of education have ensured that alternative modes of learning, differing markedly form conventional practices, have found their own place within the education framework. Non-formal education, a relatively new concept in India, is increasingly carving a niche for itself, expanding its scope and horizon beyond traditional methods of imparting knowledge.

The concept of alternative education is based on the view that society changes according to the contributions made by its members, thus widening the scope of developing creativity or social innovation, traits that are often ignored in traditional educational programmes. As such, alternative or non-formal education can not only improve the much-needed humanistic-ecological approach to education, but can also serve to be of aid to those want to avail of the benefits of adult education. The book itself however, is not simply a guide to acquaint readers with the subject of alternative education, but a comprehensive text that identifies the need for such a format of learning, and how it is redefining educational patterns. With a special focus on adult education in India, the book delineates the approaches, techniques and practices which are involved within such a mode of education, focusing upon its relevant methods, theories, trends and programmes. The focal point of alternative education is the idea of lifelong learning, a principle which also forms the base of the book's content and which has been effectively explored to comprehend the challenges and issues that confront effective adult education through alternative methods in India. The attempt is to clearly state and discuss the ways in which alternative education is, and promises to continue with the changes it has brought about in the field of education, and how Indian society at large can benefit from such educational endeavours.

It is hoped that the book serves as an insightful and thorough text for all those pursing their Masters in Education, for whom this text has been conceptualised and written.

Tushar K Sinha

Contents

1

Introduction to Non-formal Education

Human's thirst for acquiring knowledge is as old as his existence. In the early stages of life, human learnt everything by observing each and everything before him. The knowledge collected by thus are still considering priceless. Today, learning is easy because of the advent of latest technologies. We can store as much as information as we can.

Life is a continuous education process in which each of us learn something in every moment or adding new to our existing knowledge. Such kind of acquiring knowledge is known as informal education. Here, we accumulate knowledge, skills, attitudes and insights from daily experiences and exposure to the environment—at home, at work, at play; from the example and attitudes of family and friends; from travel, reading newspapers and books; or by listening to the radio or viewing films or television. Generally, informal education is unorganised and often unsystematic; yet it accounts for the great bulk of any person's total lifetime learning—including that of even a highly 'schooled' person.

Education determines a person's status in the society. But some of us are not so much lucky to get formal education. For those who had to discontinue the formational education, government is providing some facilities to educate them. Such methods are known as the non-formal education. In other words, non-formal education is defined as any organised, systematic, educational activity carried on outside the framework of the formal system to provide selected types of learning to particular subgroups in the population, adults as well as children.

Because of various reasons, people are forced to continue their formal education. So, there is a renewed interest in non-formal education (NFE) today. Formal educational systems alone cannot respond to the challenges of modern society and therefore welcomes its reinforcement by non-formal educational practices.

1.1. Evolution of Non-formal Education

Non-formal education emerged as an alternative to formal education in 1968. It was the outcome of widespread feeling that education was failing. So, the society considered the emergence of non-formal education as the best strategy to eradicate illiteracy. Most aid agencies included non-formal education in their portfolio of interventions, and the sums spent on it, were substantial. By many non-formal educations was seen as the 'ideal' form of education, far better in all respects than formal education. By others however, it came to be seen as a sub-system of education, certainly not superior and by some as considerably inferior to formal schooling. It could even be described as a temporary 'necessary evil' in situations of crisis until formal schooling could be restored.

Every country interprets non-formal education in their own way. For some, it meant every educational programme provided by the Ministry of Education apart from the schools and colleges (e.g. adult literacy classes). For others, it meant educational programmes like schooling provided by non-governmental agencies (NGOs). For yet others, it comprised all the educational and training activities of other Ministries (Women's Affairs, Health, Labour and Employment, Youth and Sports and Culture etc). Others again included within non-formal education the individualised learning programmes for different and specific learning groups—women's discussion groups, for example, programmes which approximate closely to social work and specialist counselling, whether provided by the state, NGOs, commercial agencies or other civil society bodies (religious organisations, trade unions, new social movements etc). Some took it to mean every educational activity apart from schools and colleges, including radio and television programmes, the print media (newspapers and magazines etc).

The non-formal education discourse either omitted informal education altogether or they used the term in the sense of informal learning. It divides the world of education into two, formal and non-formal, all of which is set inside a wider context of informal learning.

1.2. Concept of Lifelong Learning

Since 1986, the importance of non-formal education has been showing a recession. But today, there is a new interest in the concept of non-formal education. Now, education has changed into a lifelong process. Lifelong learning/education sees learning as taking place not simply in schools and colleges but throughout the whole of life, in many different locations and times.

The major objectives of lifelong learning/education are for helping economic growth and promoting active citizenship. To attain these objectives, the state and other agencies in non-formal education is with its contribution to these two ends.

Although, the government and other agencies give prime importance to non-formal education, it is in a state of stand still. With the increasing diversity of formal education, it is no longer clear what is and what is not included under the rubric of formal education. Moreover, the term non-formal education now covers a very wide continuum of educational programmes. At one extreme lies the flexible schooling model—national or regional sub-systems of schools for children, youth and adults. At the other extreme are the highly participatory educational programmes, hand-knitted education and training, tailor-made for each particular learning group, one-off teaching events to meet particular localised needs. Most educational programmes will of course lie somewhere between these two points. But to include both kinds of provision under the heading of non-formal education tends to lead to confusion, for they are very different in spirit and in form.

1.3. Importance of Lifelong Learning

There are numerous pressures pushing universities towards adopting lifelong learning as an educational goal. These pressures have been recognised for more than twenty years and include:

— the need to meet the expanding educational needs and expectations of larger numbers of students from increasingly diverse backgrounds

— the emergence of new occupations and careers and the rapid transformation of others
— the explosion in knowledge and technology
— the shift to an information society
— economic restructuring, organisational reform, and changes in the workplace and career patterns
— financial stringencies and the need to find more effective ways of learning and teaching within constrained resources.

Many teachers have traditionally been primarily interested in what and how much students learn and elaborate assessment methods have been devised to measure these. But in the last quarter of the twentieth century a considerable body of evidence has accumulated which suggests that we need to become much more concerned with how our students learn and the contextual forces that shape their learning.

Furthermore, assessment is integral to the notion of lifelong learning itself, for without determining what one doesn't know—which is assessment—one cannot know what needs learning. Evaluation and assessment are crucial practices in lifelong learning. Through assessment students can discover the knowledge, skills and attitudes they either lack or need to develop further. Lifelong learning begins with an appraisal of what needs to be learnt.

1.4. New Arenas

Once, the topics of adult education were determined by adults according to what they want to study so that the curriculum was built by each learning group and around their particular interests. The outcomes were not pre-set but chosen by the participants, and the evaluation was made by the participants in terms of their personal satisfaction with whether the programme met their individual needs at the time. Other learning programmes are however less highly contextualised, with pre-set outcomes, a pre-set curriculum, brought-in materials, and standardised forms of evaluation.

But in formal education, the topics will not change according to the entrance new members. An informal group is one which is highly dependent on the individual members, so that if someone joins or leaves, the nature of the group and the activities it can undertake will also change. Most groups of course lie somewhere in the middle and groups often move along the continuum in both directions.

The educational agencies set a school history curriculum. It rarely varies very much according to the interests of the class being taught. At_the other extreme lies the educational programme or activity which is made up by the facilitator/teacher in association with the participants—a creative writing course or a reading circle. The most extreme form of this kind of education and training is the single-learner provision to meet an individual need.

The position of most educational programmes of course lie somewhere between these two extremes. Most programmes will be partly formal and partly informal. Some parts of the programme will be determined by the participants, others are given by the providing agency. And most programmes will move along this continuum in both directions from time to time—going from formal to informal and from informal to formal. Both forms of education are important elements in the total learning experience. However, the term 'non-formal education' is used to cover both flexible schooling and highly participatory education. And that is the cause of the confusion which the term arouses in the minds of the listener.

All education is created on the foundation of learning. During the long process of learning, some people continue it and others discontinue. When we step into a pre-existing learning programme but mould it to our own circumstances, we are engaged in non-formal education. When we surrender our autonomy and join a programme and accept its externally imposed discipline, we are immersed in formal education.

1.5. Conclusion

Education is the wand for eradicating the darkness of ignorance. It is the way for the construction of civilised citizens. It will be inept to think that whole population in a nation gets formal education. The pressure of circumstances will throw many from the path of formal education. But life is a big educational institution. A person learns from such an institute will be a master in it. Illiteracy leads to ignorance and it further leads to exploitation. Education, whether it is formal or non-formal, is inevitable for a healthy living.

References

Aspin, D., Chapman, J., Hatton, M., and Sawano, Y. (eds.), *International Handbook of Lifelong Learning*, London: Kluwer, 2001.

Campbell, P. and Burnaby, B. (eds.), *Participatory Practices in Adult Education*, London: Erlbaum, 2001.

Coombs, P. H., *World Educational Crisis: a systems approach*, New York: Oxford University Press, 1968.

Field, J. and Leicester, M., *Lifelong Education*, London: Routledge, 2000.

Mocker, D. W. and Spear, G. E., *Lifelong Learning: formal, nonformal, informal and self-directed*, Columbus, Ohio: ERIC, 1982.

2

Types of Non-Formal Education

2.1. Introduction

Knowledge is an inevitable part of life. But some of us are not so lucky to get good education. The vicious circle of poverty, adverse circumstances, etc are the major hindrance on the path of formal education. Moreover, now, the education itself is an expensive task. Here is the importance of non-formal education.

The increasing number of students in non-formal education means that the formal education is beyond the reach of many people. There has been a rapid proliferation of 'non-formal' education programmes over the past few decades, radically altering the contours of the educational field. While the school remains the dominant educational institution in general, it is now by no means the only place where individuals can gain knowledge or can pursue explicit training objectives.

A whole range of other educational activities have developed outside the formal educational system and play a great variety of roles. Certain programmes, such as literacy campaigns, have emerged as a substitute for school education. Increasingly, though, non-formal education has come to be regarded as important for its own sake, with the growing awareness that the school is no longer capable of satisfying a whole series of increasingly diversified educational needs.

The method of non-formal education may vary country to country. But all countries, whether developed or under developed, conduct non-formal education for educating its people. There is a network which is more or less developed, consisting of a multitude of diverse educational activities, playing different roles with *de facto* relations of substitution, competition, complementarity and even sometimes opposition among themselves. This poses new challenges to the organisation and planning of education; for the techniques originally designed to plan the relatively monolithic school system are unlikely to be appropriate to a diversified educational field.

Non-formal education will not follow a predetermined syllabus. The subject for study varies from places, ages of the students, etc. Moreover different kinds of courses provided by different kinds of institution respond to different needs and serve different kinds of clientele. Each of these axes of variation can be taken as the principal defining dimension.

2.2. Classification of Non-Formal Education

The non-formal education process is not simply a method to transfer information to one another. But it is structured very thoughtfully. In particular the way in which NFE activities are described by reference to what is (not) being provided in the school system. In essence, the appellation 'non-formal' is simply a device for labelling those activities outside the control or regulation of the bureaucratic school system.

Supplementary activities providing basic, paranormal, education are widespread; once basic education is guaranteed by the school system, the focus of NFE switches to complementary activities such as vocational and, cultural education. At the same time, cutting across this 'stage theory' of the development of NFE, there is the participative approach, wherein the ideology and motivation of the providers is very different. Here NFE is seen as a positive alternative to the school system; while it typically concentrates on the provision of basic learning experiences, it is not necessarily restricted to that.

When the popular educator provides professional/vocational courses the outcome for the student, whether intended or not, is almost invariably advancement/mobility. On this basis, four forms of NFE can be distinguished by reference to their relationship with the formal school and college system. These are: paranormal education, popular education, education for personal development and professional training. They constitute four relatively autonomous segments within the educational field which differ from each other because they:

— respond to different educational needs;
— serve different clienteles;
— are being organised by different educational agencies; and, above all,
— have different relationships with the formal educational system.

This is an alternative to other classifications. Here, non-formal education is simply any organised educational activity outside the school and college mainstream: whether or not the school and college system is graded and hierarchically structured is not the issue; activities in the formal and non-formal sectors may well share the same characteristics; and so on. The point is that the activities are supplementary or, in some cases, alternative to that mainstream.

2.2.1. Paranormal Education

People discontinue education because of various reasons. Poverty is the main villain on the path of education for most of the drop outs. They are eager to acquire education. But the circumstances prevent them to go for normal school going process. Now, there are various kinds of education programmes for giving education for such people. Evening classes, official literacy programmes, distance education programmes, etc are meant for giving a second chance for such unlucky people. Some of these programmes are only a condensed form of full-time day schooling, while others are more flexible and more innovative in design and implementation. A central issue for this segment of the educational field is to guarantee equivalences with the degrees awarded in the corresponding levels of the formal school system.

The private tuition, another form of school like education, is also mushrooming. Private tutoring has a long tradition in many countries but has been booming in recent years. It has grown with the massification of formal education, as elite-and middle-class parents, who perceive their previous privileged position to be disappearing, have sought ways of retaining the competitive edge for their children. At the same times for the formal school teachers in many developing countries where civil service salaries have been seriously eroded over the last decades, the private tutoring system has been a welcome opportunity to increase their income. Demand and supply factors have therefore been reinforcing each other so as to create a real market of individual student coaching.

Private tuition constitutes a major drain on the resources potentially available to attain universal primary education. Indeed, it is interesting to note that even in a socialist country such as Hungary the offspring of a typical 'intellectuals and leaders' family in Budapest spends about one third of their total learning time in private tutoring. In Hungary, like in many other countries, the schools themselves lend their support in facilitating such extra-curricular learning opportunities. The educational and social consequences of this phenomenon have not yet been analysed.

2.2.2. Popular Education

To live in a society, people must have some basic knowledge. Such education initiatives which are explicitly directed towards the marginal groups of the population include (alternative) adult literacy projects, co-operative training, political mobilisation and community development activities. In most cases, these activities are run by voluntary organisations and stress collective development as opposed to individual competition. They are the least institutionalised sector of the diversified educational field. They take the form of informal groups, often related to churches, political parties and socio-cultural associations.

The upbringing of socially aware citizens is very important for the smooth functioning of a nation. This is very important programmes come closest to the original ideas of the enthusiastic promoters of the non-formal education in the late 60s and 70s. Because of the fluidity of this segment of the educational field, its relative importance is difficult to measure. The vitality of popular education activities seems to depend very much on the type of society and on the historical moment of its evolution.

2.2.3. Personal Development Activities

Education, which covers a whole range of learning practices organised by cultural institutions (museums, libraries, cultural centres), by clubs, circles, associations promoting leisure time activities such as astronomy, observation of the natural environment, playing music and/or listening to it, etc., by sports centres, by language institutions or even by centres of physical and mental health are coming under this group.

The learning, which is meant for the development of individuals, is the personal development activities. The increasing popularity of learning activities for personal development purposes is an indication of a profound move in the approach towards non-formal education. The development of non-formal education is largely inspired by a 'welfare approach' aiming to satisfy the demands of groups. The growing popularity of the business of private tutoring of students regularly enrolled in the school system is overshadowing these kinds of activities.

Individual demand is the regulating factor of the expansion of this educational sector. Those who have access to this educational market are mainly the elites and active urban middle classes. Even though the unemployed have much more time, they are not able to convert this into educational time and do not have the means to pay for the services being offered. This depends, of course, on the policies of providers.

Today, education is increasingly becoming a personal consumer good both for itself and to improve the quality of other consumption (e.g. learning languages for travel, etc). In sharp contrast to what is happening in the popular education where collective development is the central concern, this private market of learning is aiming at satisfying individual needs. The extent to which the parameters of this 'market' are shaped by the suppliers is unknown.

2.2.4. Professional Training

Education aims to provide a better living. For this objective, firms, trade unions, private agencies and also formal schools constitute the fourth important segment of the diversified educational field are giving professional and vocational training to the non-formal education aspirants.

Technological advancements are also changing the pattern of non-formal education sector. These changes are quite obvious in the capital market. The organisation of courses in the tertiary sector is generally cheaper than in the secondary sector. Many initiatives has began as non-formal or para-formal education, particularly in vocational training, tended to become formal and melted into the dominant educational system. But, gradually, the intrinsic value of non-formal education programmes has been recognised. School planners have realised that they can no longer answer the wide variety of educational needs and that given their highly bureaucratic organisation, schools have a limited capacity to react quickly to technological changes and new demands.

The necessity of having a multiplicity of training mechanisms and the potential of various non-formal education practices is now generally accepted. This has raised the unresolved issue of redefining the role of formal schooling vis-à-vis the other components of the educational field.

2.3. Changing Educator Styles

An educator must be flexible in order to be effective in all three types of education. An educator needs to use different leadership styles for different situations. Directive leadership may work most of the time for formal settings but democratic and non-directive (Laissez faire) styles are needed to enhance learning in nonformal and informal settings. Some educators seem to be able to adapt to the situations. Too many, however, are effective classroom teachers but less effective as nonformal educators because they try to use classroom techniques and directive leadership in both settings. Likewise, certain educators who are effective in nonformal settings lose their effectiveness when teaching in the classroom because they do not adapt to the requirements of more structure and more responsibility for learning.

Both formal and nonformal educators must be well prepared, enthusiastic, clear, and business-like in their presentations, use a variety of teaching techniques and get students involved in learning. But, the demands on educators in nonformal settings differ from those of classroom teachers. The nonformal educator must be more flexible, ready to change to meet students' diverse and changing needs. Democratic and non-directive leadership styles will be required more in nonformal settings and directive leadership will be appropriate less frequently than in the classroom.

2.4. Impact on Informal Learning

Learning by direct imitation is now recognised among the opportunities of individual, group, organised and spontaneous learning and is no longer reserved to the area of primary socialisation. There are attempts to make it more institutionalised e.g. in the eases of amateur artistic creative activity or of the situational approach to language learning. This process goes together with the rediscovery of certain modes of learning.

Knowledge and skill acquisition by direct inter-personal imitation is the best way in the most rapidly growing technologies. The dramatic rise in the popularity of learning how to use personal computers is a breath-taking example of this. The process of learning itself is more important than the result. Taking part in some collective learning-teaching experience is one way of searching for a sense of community. In the case of education of the elderly, emphasis is laid on the mental hygiene effect of the learning activity itself.

There is a growing tendency for process to dominate over product even in some professional training. Computer clubs have sprung up where software and tips are exchanged providing autonomous learning networks. The attendance of, especially office-based employees at conferences, seminars and workshops allegedly to improve their performance is breathtaking. This rapid expansion and the apparent enthusiasm of the participants in these learning experiences, raises a serious question as to the extent to which these participative styles of learning will be absorbed not only into the way non-formal education activities are organised but also into the school and college mainstream.

2.5. Conclusion

The main objective of non-formal education is to educate those who drop from schools in their early stages of life. For this, the government resort to a number of programmes which is suitable for the adult students. After a certain years, it is very difficult for the adults to go to regular educational institutions and get educated. They have to devote some time in between for getting education. In such a situation, following one type of non-formal education will not be possible. There should have a number of options to educate the illiterate.

References

Carr-Hill, R.A., *Participatory planning in education: testing some concepts,* Paris, UNESCO, Division of Education Policy and Planning (S15), 1982.

_______________ ., *The information base for the planning of the diversified education field,* Paris, IIEP/UNESCO (IIEP Research Report No.68), 1988.

Coombs P.H.; R.C. Prosser and H. Ahmed, *New paths to learning for rural children and youth,* New York, ICED, 1973.

La Belle, T.J., "Formal, non-formal and informal education: holistic perspectives on lifelong teaming". In: *International Review of Education,* 1982.

3

Need for Educational Alternatives

Communication is the privilege of human beings. We are conveying our feelings, ideas, thoughts and everything through communication. Languages developed with the growth of population. The incorrigible thirst of humans for acquiring knowledge is the beginning of education. Unfortunately, due to some adverse circumstances, many people discontinue the course of education before completion. However, they seek other methods to acquire knowledge. Such methods are known as educational alternatives. The term "alternative" is ambiguous; for some people, it implies schools for "at risk" youth only, rather than being for the education of all children and often for adults as well. So sometimes it is useful to distinguish "philosophical alternatives" from the "at-risk alternatives." These alternatives include educational options for the developmental needs and learning styles of all children.

3.1. Features of Educational Alternatives

School is the primary institution for nurturing values in one's own life. It influences a person for formulating his/her character. If a person get good living atmosphere, he/she will become a great citizen to the nation. If the educational institute is den of all wrong doings. it will also reflect in the life of a person. So, choosing a school for a child is one of the most important decisions parents make. The school—its teachers, curriculum, educational philosophy, and values both explicit and implicit—will affect the child's day-to-day life. It will help shape the child's personality, view of life, behaviour, and destiny as an adult. And it will also deeply affect the lives of the parents and the life of the family as a whole.

If the alternatives in the locality of parents are very limited, they can select it by differentiating the alternatives. In terms of commonalities, these alternatives are not hardened institutions with hardened rules or procedures. Avoiding many levels of school bureaucracies, these alternatives are flexible and warm learning communities where people come before procedures, rules, or technology.

3.1.1. Philosophical Alternatives

These are not ideal learning communities they are as susceptible to conflict, as any other organisation. Students disagree with teachers; teachers disagree with parents; parents disagree with school principals. Alternatives are unique, however, in the way in which conflict is approached and resolved, along with the value that is found within each conflict.

Philosophical alternatives are rooted in philosophies about life and learning that are fundamentally different from mainstream schooling. While these philosophies differ in many specifics, what they have in common is that they tend to not be rooted in an overly objective and rational way of knowing that causes conventional schooling to divide learning into isolated components.

At the heart of our knowledge reflects the images of self and world that will also be found in the values by which we live our lives. The teacher as the mediator between the knower and the known, the "living link in the epistemology chain," teaching a way of being in the world, a mode of relationship. Human development, then, is part and parcel with education, and includes the emotional, ecological, spiritual, physical and intellectual aspects of living. A second quality that distinguishes these alternatives from traditional schools is their long and unique history within well-rooted philosophical foundations.

The education of young human beings should involve much more than simply molding them into future workers or citizens. The education should be understood as the art of cultivating the moral, emotional, physical, psychological and spiritual dimensions of the developing child.

Conventional schooling subverts democracy by molding young people's understandings. A third quality that distinguishes alternatives from traditional education is their diversity. Unlike traditional private and public schools which are remarkably similar across time and space, most alternative schools do not subscribe to the "one model fits all communities" mentality. Each alternative creates and maintains its own methods and approaches to learning and teaching. This is a critical point that is often missed by newcomers. Each alternative approach is founded upon slightly, and sometimes drastically, different beliefs about what it means to live, learn, love, and grow in today's society.

The objective of the education is to bring up children with values. To create alternatives that are truly nurturing for children and integrated with communities, we must be conscious of the values, philosophies, and beliefs behind the systems and within ourselves. Then, rather than defending one alternative as "the answer," we can open to the idea that there is no "one best system"- just a diversity of systems that match, or do not match, with the diversity of people in the world. Further, such awareness can also enable us to change our educational systems in more conscious ways that are aligned with how we ourselves are changing. This in turn helps keep us from getting stuck in a stagnated perception of what education "should" look like.

The syllabus which is followed by a school is equally important for determining the quality of the education system of that school. Across educational alternatives, we find that traditional subjects such as reading, writing, and math are not always taught separately but integrated into students' overall learning. Other subjects like environmental education, ecology, or spirituality, not often found in more traditional school curricula, often emerge from the interests of learners and teachers in a more open-ended learning community. Yet, for the most part, subject matters are only indirectly related to the core philosophies and educational approaches used in alternative schools. In the end, what is studied matters far less than how it is learned and how it becomes relevant in students' lives.

The number of students admitted in each class is also equally important. If the number of students is less, teacher can easily handle the classes and each of the student get special attention. Small schools indicate many advantages of maintaining small schools, regardless of philosophy. In addition, many of these schools maintain a staff:student ratio that is far better than average.

3.2. Beginning of Alternative Education

Alternative education presupposes some kind of orthodoxy to which the alternative is opposed. In general, this limits the term to the last two or perhaps three centuries, with the rise of standardised and, later, compulsory education at the primary and secondary levels. In the 19th century, the Swiss humanitarian Johann Heinrich Pestalozzi; the American transcendentalists Amos Bronson Alcott, Ralph Waldo Emerson, and Henry David Thoreau; the founders of progressive education, John Dewey and Francis Parker; and educational pioneers, such as Maria Montessori and Rudolf Steiner; among others, all insisted that education should be understood as the art of cultivating the moral, emotional, physical, psychological, and spiritual aspects of the developing child. Anarchists such as Leo Tolstoy and Francisco Ferrery Guardia emphasised education as a force for political liberation, secularism, and elimination of class distinctions.

More recently, social critics such as John Caldwell Holt, Paul Goodman, Frederick Mayer, George Dennison and Ivan Illich have examined education from more individualist, anarchist, and libertarian perspectives, that is, critiques of the ways that they feel conventional education subverts democracy by molding young people's understandings. Other writers, from the revolutionary Paulo Freire to American educators like Herbert Kohl and Jonathan Kozol, have criticised mainstream Western education from the viewpoint of their varied left-liberal and radical politics.

3.3. Forms of Alternative Education

Education can be divided in to three, primary, secondary and tertiary. A wide variety of educational alternatives exist at these three levels. These generally fall into four major categories:

i) school choice,

ii) alternative school,

iii) independent school, and

iv) home-based education.

These general categories can be further broken down into more specific practices and methodologies.

3.3.1. School Choice

School is the first platform for students to acquire knowledge. If the foundation is strong, the remaining part of education will also be safe. School choice describes programmes that allow students to choose to attend any of various participating private and public schools, usually based on a system of vouchers, tax credits, or scholarships. These programmes are generally intended to give parents more input in which primary and secondary schools their children attend. The goal of school choice is to create competition between schools for education.

The competitive spirit enables parents to choose a school that provides a Christian or Biblically based worldview in their children's instruction; stronger discipline; better foundational skills including reading, writing, mathematics, and science; everyday skills from handling money to farming, or other desirable foci, which the parent perceives as important, but neglected.

If parents were given a choice where public funding should go, they would pick the better schools and under-performing schools would have to improve or lose funding. The school should be the focus of reform. Some school choice proponents hold that if a school is failing the student, it should be replaced.

Since children from impoverished families almost exclusively attend public schools, a voucher system would allow these students to opt out of bad schools and acquire a better education, thereby granting the decision-making power to students and their parents, not school administrators. This would level the playing field by broadening opportunities for low-income students to attend as good of schools as the middle classes instead of the current two-tiered system which educates the middle and upper classes, but not the lower classes, particularly minorities.

Due to the expanded market and subsequent demand for privately run schooling, a myriad of schools of varying selectivity and philosophies would arise to meet this demand, providing greater choice than the publicly run school system. The choice of schools would be analogous to the choice of food products in a supermarket, only limited by physical constraints and not government budgets. Supporters also argue that having a greater number of schools from which students can choose would reduce overcrowding and allow students to attend schools that best meet their learning styles and needs.

The decentralisation or localisation of power endemic to privately run schooling would facilitate greater parent teacher interaction, as the teachers would be accountable to parents, not to a distant city or state board. A close-knit community of students, parents, and faculty unified by a common ideal would promote involvement among the relevant parties. Effectively, proponents of school choice argue, vouchers would confer the benefits of privately run schooling on a wide swath of the population while lessening, or even negating the cost.

Instead of government forcing school choice, citizens and parents need to become more aware of who runs the schools, and for laws to help improve that awareness. Any head of the school board who values their position will likely do everything possible to ensure the school runs better, if citizens are more active in deciding who stays or goes. Supporters of school choice sometimes say that even if the school board were perfect, one school, generally, cannot educate the myriad of different students any more than one company could meet the needs of all consumers.

3.3.2. Alternative School

When the educational establishment and curriculum follows nontraditional method, it is an alternative school. These schools have a special curriculum offering a more flexible programme of study than a traditional school. A wide range of philosophies and teaching methods are offered by alternative schools; some have strong political, scholarly, or philosophical orientations, while others are more ad-hoc assemblies of teachers and students dissatisfied with some aspect of mainstream or traditional education.

The alternative high school is any junior high school, high school, senior high school, or secondary school having a special curriculum offering a more flexible programme of study than a traditional school. An alternative high school serves as an addition to a larger traditional junior high school, high school, senior high school, or secondary school.

Alternative education covers all forms of non-traditional educational methods and philosophies, including school choice, independent school, homeschooling, and alternative high school. However, even the narrower usage of the term may refer to a range of school type such as a school with an innovative and flexible curriculum aimed at bright, self-motivated students; a school intended to accommodate students with behavioral problems; or a school with special remedial programmes.

3.3.2.1. An 'Alternative' to Prevent Drop Outs

Education offers a better perspective and means for living. But many people are forced to discontinue their education due to various reasons. Individuals dropping out of school will have their lives impacted both personally and professionally. Society will also contend with the possible negative outcomes where supporting the individual in the long term may be required. Especially concerning are potential drop out rates of students with disabilities. Special education dropout rates nationally have been on the decline. Still the statistics are staggering. Addressing the problem of dropout rates brings to the forefront a myriad of causes and forces examination of the issue with special attention to framing the problem.

The concept, alternative education helps to provide education for school dropouts. Schools operated within Educational Services Commissions can offer the "small school" approach to help high risk, special education students who have been placed in the alternative school due to difficulties in typical classroom settings. Counselling services are employed to build better behavioural coping skills. In the high stakes world of alternative education, administrators are confronted with questions of personal and organisational failure should a student drop out of school. Although it is the nature of the business, special education students dropping out of school can be regarded the ultimate failure.

When a special education student drops out at a small alternative school the ripple effect is felt throughout the school. Therefore considering the causes and implementing prevention programmes becomes especially important. Students of special education may feel less confident with years of learning frustration, finding it "easier" to quit rather than keep "struggling." Associated with this frustration, behaviour becomes less consistent and life choices made from that point of view can produce negative outcomes. High risk behaviors stemming from poor self esteem may include addiction related issues, gang involvement and crime activity engagement. Also related to these issues could be the pregnancy rate, where young mothers fail to return to school.

The rate of drop outs will also be influenced by a student's family income and socioeconomic status as well as the educational achievement level of a parent. Children can be faced with family dysfunction issues such as neglect, caregivers facing addiction issues or other family members dropping out of school. Other considerations range from students having to support their families to issues related to personal safety in the community / or home. These risk factors are not the only ones faced by today's young people but have been considered "valid" reasons for students dropping out. Students may also drop out for child care related issues, criminal involvement or even incarceration. Finally, the psychiatric issues students face may lead to long term hospitalisations which cause students to inevitably drop out.

The fundamental truth is that students who drop out of school "disengage" from instruction and the overall school environment. For special education students defining the causes of this disengagement are critical. The No Child Left Behind Act signed January 8, 2002 requires educators to be prove adequate yearly progress to decrease dropout rates. The Individuals with Disabilities Act in 1997 and 2004 also require schools to reduce dropout rates.

Schools are unable to respond effectively with their current level of resources beyond a certain point of adaptation. In some cases the problem simply goes away as students drop out, thus freeing the school of any more responsibility to change its internal structure. To control the number of school dropouts, it is important to find out the underlying causes. Through investigation of controversial issues, identifying solutions that would be first mutable and reduce drop out rates of students with disabilities is not a simplistic process. Through various support groups, outside agency support and family outreach, family and personal issues can be addressed. To supplement services, releases signed with outside psychiatric professionals, enable school counselors to develop counseling goals for students. Schools exploring teen pregnancy issues can utilise Planned Parenthood for educational seminars.

The school drop out can also be prevented by examining curricula. Students must find meaningful, relevant culture within the school to engage in the curriculum. Further, engagement is promoted when students feel drawn to the school climate, identifying with the mission through school activities. Developing activity that promotes cohesion in the alternative school would be found in a School to Work Programme.

The teacher training must also be every effective. Drop out prevention programmes usually focus on the individual, not the organisation. If teaching is ineffective, students can not improve academically, thus promoting disengagement. Improving teaching skills and mastery is the one true aspect the school can control. Improvement in skill delivery and curriculum connection can be accomplished with special attention on teacher training and ongoing curriculum evaluation. Extensive information is available on improving teaching in the special education setting. However, from the "disengagement" lens, instruction must be effective and address the complexities that contribute to dropping out in the alternative school.

It is worse to do nothing. Focusing blame on the individual is unacceptable. Although personal choices play a role in dropping out of school, educators must be prepared to examine their organisation and players within to manage the challenge. From that perspective, administrators and teachers can build "active engagement," in mission building in the alternative school approaches to better serve at risk students.

3.3.2.2. *Popular education*

The political decisions have greater influence on education. The absence of broadminded views of the politicians often put education at risk. The politicians try to passes wrong perspective to the younger generations through education. Popular education is at the crossroads between politics and pedagogy, and strongly relies on the democratic ideal of the Enlightenment, which considered public education as a main tool of individual and collective emancipation.

Popular education is an educational technique designed to raise the consciousness of its participants and allow them to become more aware of how an individual's personal experiences are connected to larger societal problems. Participants are empowered to act to effect change on the problems that affect them.

3.3.3. Independent School

Schools function without any external support is known as independent school. It is a school which is not dependent upon national or local government for financing its operation and is instead operated by tuition charges, gifts, and in some cases the investment yield of an endowment. Independent schools may have a religious affiliation, but the more precise usage of the term excludes parochial schools and other schools with financial dependence upon outside organisations.

3.3.4. Home-Based Education

When the students get education from parents or guardians, rather than in a public or private school, such education is known as home based education. Prior to the introduction of compulsory school attendance laws, most childhood education occurred within the family or community, with only a small portion of the population attending schools or employing tutors or governesses. Currently, the great majority of children in developed nations receive their formal education in public and private schools.

Home schooling is a legal option for parents who wish to provide their children with a different learning environment than exists in nearby schools. Some of these families make this choice on religious grounds. Many do it because of a dissatisfaction with the schools in their area or with the institutional effect of school in general. It is also an alternative for families living in isolated rural locations and those who choose, for practical or personal reasons, not to have their children attend school.

3.4. Alternative Schooling in India

India followed the custom of Gurukula in education. But from the early 20th century, many educational theorists in India discussed and implemented radically different forms of education. Rabindranath Tagore's Shantiniketan and Mahatma Gandhi's ideal of "basic education" are prime examples. In recent years many new alternative schools have formed, such as Sarang, Palakad Kerala, Adharshila Saakad MP, Poorna Learning Centre and Sita School—Bangalore, Kanavu, and Timbaktoo Collective. In the last few decades holistic education, in which the environment of the student is considered an essential part of the educational process, has become popular.

The Gurukula education or the traditional system of Indian learning is now regarded as a basis for developing new methods of alternative schooling. In this traditional system, students used to stay in "Gurukulas," where they received free food, shelter and education. A "guru" used to teach the students. Progress was not based on examinations and marks; tests were given by the Gurus but not ranks. This system used to nurture the students' natural creativity and all-round personality development.

The mainstream education system in India is still based on the traditional education system. A few projects aim to rejuvenate the early education system are Prabodhini Gurukula, Veda Vijnana Gurukulam and Maitreyi Gurukulam, etc.

Lord Macaulay was the proponent of this system. Many students in these and similar projects take up research work in the field of Sanskrit studies, Vedic studies, Vedic science, Yoga and Ayurveda. Others after completing their education in a Gurukula continue into regular mainstream education such as Bachelor degrees in Commerce, Science, Engineering, etc. Students coming to these studies from Gurukulas are regarded as more brilliant and creative than those who have studied in the regular education system.

3.5. Trend in Alternative Education

There are a number of trends in education-at-large that directly relate to approaches for learning and teaching which are used in both traditional and alternative settings. These trends relate most closely to the transactional and transformational orientations.

— *Character education*: Attention to qualities of the students' being and acting in society that often focuses on more intrapersonal and interpersonal aspects of student development.

— *Cooperative learning*: Working with students in groups so that the students learn more about working together rather than just independently.

— *Developmental education*: Focus on a child's growth across life stages, may include physical, intellectual, psychological, and/or spiritual development.

— *Experiential learning*: It means merely learning by doing and it can be incorporated into any philosophical approach or hodgepodge of educational practices.

— *Learning styles*: Refers to how each student often shows preferences for using various modes of learning such as learning best by reading, by hearing, or by moving their bodies. There are many ways to "cut the pie" for describing different learning styles.

3.6. Conclusion

Poverty, illiteracy and unemployment are the evils in any country. Every individual dreams to lead a very good life. Education is the way of a better life but the circumstances are not favourable for most of the people to decent education. To uplift the standard of living, the government and many non-governmental organisations conduct alternative education to help those who are not lucky to get a regular education process.

References

Gregg, S., "Creating effective alternatives for disruptive students", *Clearing House*, 1999.

Guerin, G. & Denti, L., "Alternative education support for youth at-risk", *Clearing House*, 1999.

Lange, C.M., "Characteristics of alternative schools and programs serving at-risk students", *High School Journal*, 1998.

Rutherford, R.B., Jr. & Quinn, M.M., "Special education in alternative education programs", *Clearing House*, 1999.

Sagor, R., "Equity and excellence in public schools: the role of the alternative school", *Clearing House*, 1999.

4

Organisation and Planning of Non-formal Education

The formal education system is a systematic process. But the informal education does not follow any such process. However, for the effective implementation of non-formal education, the organisation and planning is a must. The diversification of the educational activities has been accompanied by a process of diversification of the organising agencies and a proliferation of clienteles. Out-of-school education is synonymous of private initiative. The state is an important actor in the educational diversification process.

The non-formal education programmes are undertaken by the ministries of culture, labour, industries, agriculture, etc. Local authorities are also taking an increasing share of the organisation of various learning activities, mainly, but not exclusively, in the non-professional areas.

4.1. Non-Governmental Sector

Conducting non-formal education is the major activity of the non-governmental sector. They provide three main types of non-formal education activities such as: the enterprises, the non profit-making organisations, and the profit-making institutions.

But organising training programmes are the privilege of big enterprises which can mobilise the required resources for this purpose. In many cases, the enterprises of the same branch or even of different branches pull together in order to create special institutions which provide them with the required training services.

The non-profit sector covers a wide variety of organising agencies. There are large organisations such as trade unions and churches which have broad social or religious aims and use NFE as one of their multiple activities to promote those broader aims. There are also other large organisations with a national coverage but which pursue explicit cultural and educational aims. There are finally a multitude of small socio-cultural associations which are the result of local level initiatives.

Diversity is the objective of profit making sector also. But here, the range varies from big multi-national training companies (e.g. for language courses) at one extreme to the individual tutoring at the other extreme.

4.2. Target Audience

Education is the minimum requirement for the development of a nation. So, educating the youth is the need of a government and it is the most important organiser of paranormal education. It is also very much present in professional training and, to a lesser extent, in training for personal development. It is only marginally taking part in popular education.

The enterprises are clearly concentrating on professional training although they might also get involved in some training activities aimed at the personal development of their employees. The non profit-making organisations are mainly involved in popular education activities. But in certain cases the trade unions may also run important professional training programmes while various large- and small-scale voluntary organisations may also be involved in personal development activities. Finally, the profit-making institutions are mainly active in the area of professional and personal development training.

4.3. Competition and Complementarity

The objective of the different agencies involved in the non-formal education sector is to educate the illiterate and the school drop outs. Even though there are lots of agencies involved in these activities, there is no overlapping or competition between them. In fact, different organisers are often serving different client groups. The government generally follows a welfare approach. Its various training programmes are mainly directed towards the lower strata of the society who cannot pay fees and have relatively low standards of education.

The churches and several militant voluntary organisations provide popular education activities to the marginal groups of the society in shanty towns and in backward rural areas, while the trade unions offer the same type of activities and some others to the members of their organisations who already have employment and are therefore relatively better off. In the personal development sector, similar distinctions can be made between the popular clientele that takes part in state controlled activities, the clients of better means who can afford private courses and the members of social organisations - such as trade unions - who can take part in cheap courses offered by their respective organisations. In the professional training sector, the main distinction is between the public sector and the others. The public sector is the only organiser responding to the needs of the uneducated and unemployed.

The enterprises concentrate on those who are already employed and have a fair level of basic education. The private institutions are focusing on those who can pay, that is to say on the non-manual workers and especially on those employed in the tertiary sector of the economy.

Education doesn't mean that it is a learning by reading books. At the same time, it provides some practical knowledge also. However, there are programmes where teaching activities take place at some institution but use laboratory and shop facilities of other institutions, perhaps in enterprises. Some are promoted by one kind of institution (co-operative, trade union) and funded by another, while teaching materials and programmes may be provided by a third. There is also an important process of subcontracting between the public and the private sector, and also between the institutions within the same sector.

4.4. Enrolementing and Subcontracting Procedures in Non-formal Education

It is sometimes difficult to make clear distinctions between the enrolments in different institutions and more generally to evaluate because of the main interlinkages and subcontracting procedures which exist between different institutions.

4.4.1. Age

Age is an important factor in non-formal education. There are lots of people who not even go to the school even once. But mostly, children are forced to discontinue education because of poverty. Conflicts in homes and the character of the students are also major factors. However, the age group of most of the students for non-formal education is 15-24. For many youngsters NFE offers a second chance for obtaining certificates corresponding to the various levels of formal schooling. Moreover, many people tend to complete their knowledge and skills by taking NFE courses immediately after the completion of a given level of formal education.

4.4.2. Gender

All most all countries, women get very less opportunities for education. The social set up, mentality of the people, family problems, etc are prevent them to mingle in a society and get education. People believe that educating their girl child is the wastage of money and they refrain from formal education. Now, the concept of people has changed a lot. But still, the conditions of most of the women are the same.

The percentage of women participating in FE varies according to the economic and socio-cultural characteristics of the countries. In many developing countries, the male participants outnumber the female ones. As far as one thirds of adult education as providing second chance opportunities to those who have missed out, and women predominate in that category, the low female participation rates in many developing countries is a rather disturbing finding. NF education does not seem to be able to correct the main gender disparities which are being reproduced by the formal school system.

4.4.3. Socio-Professional Categories

People who have benefited more from formal education also benefit more from non-formal education. Non-formal education programmes are concentrated in the urban areas. Enterprises offer courses to those who are already employed, while various social organisations such as trade unions, co-operative associations, etc. reserve their training programmes for their respective members.

Commercial institutions select their clients on the basis of their capacity to pay fees.

4.4.4. Region

Religion has an important role in educating the people. Some religious organisations encourage the formal education while the others prevent some people. Today, a lot of religious agencies are working in the non-formal education sector to educate the illiterate.

4.5. Diversification of Education

The classical ethos of non-formal education offer second chance educational opportunities and possibilities for social promotion to the poor. Programmes which come close to this ideal are the mass literacy programmes in developing countries. The participants in these do indeed tend to be poor rural women, it is the slightly better off among them who succeed.

Non-formal education also provides opportunities for further professional and personal development to those who have already a minimum level of formal education and a decent position in the society. Manifestly, the recent rapid expansion of the out-of-school educational activities has been of more benefit to those who follow the second track.

The main driving force behind the diversification process has not been an irresistible movement towards more equality but rather the objective world-wide necessity to adapt educational practice to the requirements of the rapid technological, economic and social changes. Moreover, there might well be a danger that any 'extra' resources, both of institutions and of personnel will tend to be mopped up by courses for non-vocational personal development for the same middle classes.

Because of unprecedented technological innovations, the knowledge generated in an individual's lifetime surpasses in quantity the knowledge to be learned from preceding ages. This has resulted in an increased social pressure for learning not only in the professional sphere but also in the daily life sphere. At the same time, the reduction of working hours has led to an increase in leisure time which, in turn, is at the origin of the impressive development of the whole sector of learning for personal development purposes. Furthermore, the revolutionary expansion of learning possibilities brought about by new techniques of communication and the increase in spending power of at least the better off strata of the population are additional factors tending to promote the process of educational diversification in a particular direction.

4.6. Conclusion

Non-formal education is the outcome of a thoughtful effort and it should be carried out without fail for the benefit of the society. The repercussions of non formal education should be visible in almost all spheres of life and so, planning should be made accordingly. There are a number of organisations working in the field of non formal education for providing a better perspective to its people. But at the same time government should also provide adequate support and proper guidance for the success of their endurances.

References

Carr-Hill, R.A., "Participatory planning in education: testing some concepts", Paris, *UNESCO*, Division of Education Policy and Planning (S15), 1982.

_______________., "The information base for the planning of the diversified education field", Paris, *IIEP/UNESCO (IIEP Research Report No.68)*, 1988.

La Belle, T.J., "Formal, non-formal and informal education: holistic perspectives on lifelong teaming", In: *International Review of Education*, Vol. 28, 1982.

5

Non-Formal Education in India

5.1. Introduction

In older ages, India followed a system of Gurukula in education and it was the prerogative of the upper class people. But, India realised the importance of education under British rule and it started aggressive education programmes. Non-formal education in India has developed a restricted meaning of an alternative delivery system of education for children who are not able to participate in the formal elementary school. Non-formal education has therefore, been limited to providing a second chance to those children who are out-of- school. Such children are often described as drop-outs. However, a very large number of such children are, in fact, pull-outs from school because of economic and cultural compulsions. Many children may be called stay-outs because the reach of the primary school system in India is not universal. Besides pull-outs and stay-outs, a very large number of children are what may be termed as push-outs. These children do not find the primary school attractive or meaningful.

Indian constitution aims to provide free and compulsory education to all children up to the age of 14. But, for a variety of reasons the formal school system has tended to leave out millions of rural and urban poor children who are not able to attend a full time day-school. Consequently, there is a need for developing a viable alternative system of education which would provide basic education for all children in the country. Non-formal education has evolved as one such alternative.

With a vision to educate all, Indian government started non-formal education as an alternative to formal elementary education in 1976. During this period, nine educationally backward states in the country were persuaded to initiate experimental NFE centres. In 1988, following the introduction of the National Policy on Education, a full- fledged scheme of non-formal education supported by the Central Government was introduced primarily in ten educationally backward states, as well as all over the country in urban slums, remote areas, desert and hilly regions.

The scheme of non-formal education envisaged wide spread participation by state governments as well as voluntary agencies engaged in educational programmes, specially in rural and tribal areas.

5.2. Present Scenario of Non-formal Education

Socio-economic constraints are the main hindrance on the path of most of the children. These include working children who assist in domestic, chores, like fetching fuel, fodder, water, attend to siblings, graze cattle, etc, children from scattered habitations with population below the permissible school norms drop outs. Any strategy for UEE must, therefore, take into account alternative strategies to reach this important but marginalised group of children.

The government of India introduced National Policy on Education (NPE) in 1986 and the Programme of Action in 1992 as a call for a large systematic programme of non-formal education (NFE) as an integral component of the strategy to achieve universalisation of elementary education. Through NFE, India aims to educate of out-of-school children. Although planned and concerted efforts in non-formal education is barely two and half decades old in India, it has travelled a long way from the early beginnings in 1970s to a full-fledged scheme of the Government of India reaching out to nearly seven million children in the age group 6-14.

The NFE programme, which seeks to provide out-of-school children with opportunities for primary education, was under NCERT in early seventies and was later initiated as a centrally sponsored scheme in 1978. It was originally available in nine educationally backward states viz, Andhra Pradesh, Assam, Bihar, Jammu and Kashmir, M.P., Orissa, Rajasthan, U.P., and West Bengal. Later it was extended to Arunachal Pradesh and the educationally backward pockets of the remaining States.

While reiterating the guidelines regarding NFE in the National Policy on Education, 1986 and its Programme of Action (POA) the 8th Plan envisaged that NFE will be developed as a complementary system to the formal elementary education system. It stressed the importance of making necessary investments in qualitative improvement of NFE and reiterated that the advantages of NFE lay in its flexibility, and adaptability to the needs of an important minority of children.

As per the 8th Plan, the central government should continue to play a crucial role for provision of funds for NFE till this complementary system of elementary system gets firmly established. The share of central assistance for mixed NFE projects should be enhanced to 75% and there need not be any rigid proportion between mixed and the girls centres. Financial assistance may be restricted to educationally backward States and educationally backward districts in non-educationally backward States.

5.2.1. Changing Scenario of Primary Education

There was a national awake among Indians to acquire basic education in the shortest possible time since 1986. Several programmes of support to primary and elementary education in the country have been initiated in order to achieve this goal. The experience gathered since 1976 and particularly since 1988 in the area of non-formal education clearly demonstrates that universal elementary education can only be achieved if non-formal education is made available as a viable alternative to formal school education.

The success of NFE programme was limited, but it has become acceptable to a large section of the rural poor parents who are keen and willing to send their children to school but find the formal full- day school not suitable in their economic condition. The feasibility of non-formal education has become enhanced in the last eight years.

5.2.1.1. Lok Jumbish Project

To achieve universalisation of elementary education through a community based and decentralised approach, the state of Rajasthan introduced Lok Jumbish Project (LJP) in 1992. The project commenced with support of SIDA, GOI & GOR in the proportion of 3:2:1 has taken up non-formal education as one of the strategies for achieving UEE in rural areas of the State. Currently the programme covers about 20,000 children through approximately 1000 NFE centres. The programme was a feasible design for providing primary education to out-of-school children who are working or have crossed the school admission age.

5.2.1.1. Shiksha Karmi Project

Shiksha Karmi Project (SKP) in Rajasthan was the largest experiment in non-formal and alternative education outside the centrally sponsored NFE scheme. It was launched in year 1987 with the assistance of SIDA to revitalise and expand primary education in the remote, inaccessible and backward villages of Rajasthan. The SKP has utilised the services of local youth who are specially selected and are trained rigorously and regularly, to revitalise primary schools in the most difficult areas of the State.

SKP provide non-formal Education to out of school children in the age group 6-14 years who are unable to attend day school due to socioeconomic and cultural constraints. It is obligatory for every shiksha karmi to run a PP in his/her village outside school hours, in addition to running a day school during regular school hours.

SKP also aims to educate young girls who cannot travel long distances to attend either day school. A local person, preferably a woman, is selected to run such programme in her own home after necessary training and provision of other inputs.

The non-formal education programmes are very successful in providing primary education to out of school children in educationally backward areas has been by and large accepted and validated. However, NFE is subject to criticism in certain quarters as a low cost inferior and ineffective alternative for full time school. NFE seeks to legitimise child labour as it is based on the assumption that poor and deprived children must work and, therefore, cannot attend regular schools. Nevertheless it cannot be denied that despite numerous shortcomings, NFE has provided access to primary education for millions of children in remote and inaccessible rural areas and urban slums, specially girls, and disadvantaged sections of society.

NFE may be seen as an evolving model emerging from existing socioeconomic realities. Where it has been effectively and properly implemented, NFE has been useful as a stepping stone for formal schooling, in addition to improving the self esteem, confidence and social skills of children. A few voluntary organisations have been able to provide vocational inputs to NFE thereby improving the employment prospects of children. More importantly, NFE is recognised as an alternative by parents and the community. Currently, the NFE programme has the potential of enrolling nearly half the number of children enrolled in the formal school system. Together, the formal primary school and NFE can fulfill the demand for primary education for all children in the country in the age group 6-11.

Due to insufficient funding, inappropriate organisational structures, inefficient operationalisation, inadequate involvement of the local community and unrealistic expectations of completion of primary schooling in two years by working children through part-time instruction imparted by under-equipped and low paid para teachers, the NFE programme has not emerged as a credible alternative to the primary school system. Development of appropriate curricula as well as suitable teaching learning materials for the NFE clientele and recurring training of instructors/supervisors have not received adequate attention. Earnest and effective implementation of NFE by states is also generally lacking.

The programme of NFE has had to operate in the most difficult conditions. Aimed at out-of-school children, the programme generally addresses first generation learners who comet from economic and socially backward sections of the society. These children have, by and large, no educational or literacy background within the family.

Furthermore, the programme is implemented largely in rural areas, often in remote regions especially in tribal areas. It has not always been possible to provide the essential facilities which are a pre-condition for the success of the programme. At the same time, it is difficult to retain functionaries within the programme for any extended period of time because of the paltry honorarium which has been a subject of widespread concern and repeated criticism. Even the small sum of money often does not reach the

Instructors on time leading to not only discontentment but also disruption of NFE centres. This leads to discontinuity and wastage. Training of Instructors, Supervisors and Project Officers have been inadequate and sporadic. MLL based, local specific curriculum for NFE learners has not been developed in most of the States/UTs.

5.3. Non-Formal Education Department in the NCERT

The non-formal education programmes flourished since 1988, when a full-fledged department of NFE was established in the NCERT. Prior to 1988, NFE functioned as part of other departments. With the establishment of a department, NFE became recognised as an alternative to elementary education. From 1988-1995 the department was also given the responsibility of overseeing education to scheduled castes and scheduled tribes since NFE emphasised reaching these communities where large number of children were out-of-school. In 1995, the department was re-organised and renamed department of education in non-formal and alternative schooling. This reorganisation has vindicated the significance of NFE as an essential alternative to formal elementary education. The department is now poised to play a significant role in the achievement of universal elementary education which has been a goal for the country.

5.31. Functions of the Department

The department of NFE introduced a number of activities. Following the 1988 central scheme of non-formal education, the department was designated as a national resource centre for non-formal education. The functions and roles of the department included:

— Providing academic and technical support to state agencies as well as voluntary agencies implementing the scheme of non-formal education;

— Evolving training models and providing training for functionaries in non-formal education at all levels;-

— Developing materials and methodologies for the implementation of non-formal education;

— Conducting fundamental and action research in all aspects of non-formal education;

— Providing extension services to all agencies (state as well as voluntary) concerned with non-formal education;

— Carrying out programme in pupil evaluation in non-formal education; and

— Creating and maintaining capacities at the state level for successful implementation of the scheme of non-formal education.

The department has carried out numerous activities and has attempted to create academic and technical capacities in the states and amongst the voluntary agencies implementing non-formal education.

5.3.2. NFE in District Level

The success of any programme depends on the obtainability and the NFE is also the same. A critical analysis of activities and developments at the district level singled out this aspect as the most crucial factor for NFE implementation strategies. In number of cases there were communication gaps between district education officers and assistant directors/coordinators (NFE). In some districts this created impediments in effective programme implementation. In view of this, the department organised a series of orientation courses for district education officers including block education officers connected with the NFE programme.

For the effective implementation, these programmes generated a climate for open dialogue between the administrative functionaries and the programme organisers. As an outcome of this the support system was forthcoming in favour of joint efforts towards meeting the challenges faced at the grassroots level.

5.4. Training Methods

In non-formal education, the teachers should handle the students of different age group and so, there character also will be very different. To educate such a community, the teachers must be specially trained. The enrolment, participation and achievement level of NFE children from schedule castes and schedule tribes are still significantly low. There are a number of factors that continue to arrest the educational developments and interventions. The crucial areas of concern are low level of efficiency of instructors, very little relevance of instructional materials to cultural and socioeconomic contexts of these communities. The teaching-learning processes are largely not connected with the learning style of SC/ST learners. The educational process inadequately reflects tie cultural environment of these special group of learners.

The teachers should be trained to develop basic skills and should know the socio-cultural contexts of the communities. The programmes were intended to help the key resource persons and instructors to adopt suitable approaches and transactional strategies for creating a joyful learning climate in the NFE centres.

5.4.1. Regional Language Literacy Initiatives

The uplift of regional language is the priority of every government. The government policy lays special emphasis on the voluntary organisations for evolving innovative designs for effective implementation of the centrally sponsored NFE Scheme.

Teaching should be done by understanding the need of the area. There are a large number of voluntary organisations in the country who have taken the lead in the development of environment-based and area-based teaching-learning materials and teaching-learning processes. Some of these organisations, in their endeavour to renew their instructional materials, requested the department in providing academic guidance in the material preparation work.

Different areas have different needs and problems. In response to this the department organised working group meetings for review and finalisation of five primers developed by three leading organisations of Bihar, Rajasthan and West Bengal, namely Samanvaya Ashram, Bodhgaya; Gandhi Vidya Mandir, Sardarshahar, Rajasthan; and Indian Association of Adult Education, West Bengal branch.

5.4.2. Literacy Mission among Street and Working Children

The biggest menace of India is the uncontrollable growth of street and working children. Mostly, the street children remain the part of street and they are vulnerable to criminal activities. Designing educational programmes for street and working children is one of the critical areas of curriculum concern in the country. Based on the philosophies and focus of various organisations both at the government and NGO levels a number of strategies were adopted. Consequently, a variety of materials were developed under different educational designs.

It is the duty of the government to curtail the street population. If they are given good education and training, the government can solve this problem in a certain extend. Now, there are lots of initiatives to educative the street and working children. For this, general and core skills have been identified. The development of learner-specific skill oriented instructional package related to different occupational groups in the urban and rural set-up is in progress.

5.4.3. Supporting Materials for NFE Programme

The non availability of teaching material is the biggest problem before the NFE children. They get very limited exposure with regard to teaching-learning materials. In some pockets the text-books are the only reading materials before them. Being working children, the learners come to NFE centre after day's hard work. The NFE approach lays special emphasis in providing a congenial and joyful learning climate in the classroom. The local specific material series were planned to meet this gap areas.

During 1992-93 the department made special intervention in this regard for the development of a series of supplementary reading materials based on local specific materials in the form of stories, games, riddles, jokes and-anecdotes, proverbs loaded with messages, poems and songs popularly sung during festivals and celebrations.

To explore the various types of local specific materials available in different cultural settings and linguistic groups, the department organised four regional level planning meetings. In this regard a set of criteria and tools were developed for identification, collection, classification, scrutiny and refinement of local specific materials from different sources. In the planning meetings the modalities and available sources were identified and the tools finalised. In this task a large number of faculty members from district resource units, DIETs, NFE instructors, primary school teachers, project officers, supervisors, teacher educators and the SCERT faculty members were oriented in the processes of identification and development of local specific materials.

Materials available in regional languages are more useful for the NFE students. So, the department converted the selected materials into small booklets in Hindi. The large amount of materials collected from different sources was classified, categorised on the basis of the criteria laid down for this. The materials were scrutinised, selected and modified. These were presented in the form of small books. In all there are a set of six books on games, stories, songs and poems, proverbs, riddles and jokes. Similar sets of books were developed with the help of materials collected from Karnataka, Andhra Pradesh, and Kerala.

Under this programme, the states and voluntary organizations also got a good opportunity to collect a rich resource material. The project work evinced keen interest among the functionaries of different organisations both at the government and voluntary organisation levels for generating a rich resource-base through collection of local specific materials from different sources. States like Bihar, Rajasthan and Andhra Pradesh have developed a series of local specific materials on the basis of cultural components of their own States. These States have made experimentation in the use of these materials in the teaching-learning process in various group- learning situations. Some of the Primers developed by these organisations have integrated the local specific components in a creative way.

5.4.4. Supporting Reading Materials for Social Integration

Adult education aims to achieve economic development, social integration and environmental protection. NFE learners belong to socially and educationally deprived communities. There is little scope for getting experiences in education for social and emotional integration. To meet this gap area the department took-up a project in 1989-1990 for the development of supplementary reading materials pertaining to this area. In this connection the department reviewed the available supplementary reading materials that promote the values of social, emotional and national integration. The analysis helped the department in identifying seven potential themes.

5.4.5. Manuals for Training

Upgradation of capabilities of NFE functionaries at various levels is one of the significant responsibilities of the department. The department, through a series of discussion sessions, developed the instructor's manual in Hindi. This was developed in a modular form. The various chapters were well integrated with each other. At the same time there was an element of flexibility. Each chapter was a self-contained unit and presented in terms of issues related to day-to-day responsibilities and functions of the NFE Instructors working in various settings. The entire manual was written in a very simple language that would be easily understandable by NFE instructors even with limited background.

The Hindi manuals were rendered into 13 regional languages namely, Assamese, Bengali, Gujarati, Kannada, Manipuri, Marathi, Malyalam, Oriya, Punjabi, Telugu, Tamil, Urdu and Konkini. The regional language versions of the manuals were also tried-out and edited with the help of state level functionaries by dovetailing different local specific situations and cultural components of the concerned States to ensure relevance and functionality of the manuals.

The NCERT published only the Hindi and Urdu manuals. The regional versions were got printed by the State Level agencies. The department has got a rich feedback on the various chapters of the Manuals. On the basis of the feedback and experiences gained over the last eight years the department now intends to review and add some further dimensions in the manuals keeping in view the emerging trends. In the context of Education for all, the DPEP States are putting forward a demand for academic support from the department in the adaptation of the training manuals, keeping in view the State specific contexts.

5.4.6. Growth of Middle Level NFE Programme

There is provision in the NFE Scheme for implementing NFE Programmes at two levels, namely, Primary and Middle. In the first phase of launching of the NFE programme the scheme laid special emphasis on the primary level NFE centres. Consequently, a number of experimentation and innovative programmes related to Primary level NFE Programmes were initiated by the States and Voluntary Organisations during the VII and VIII Five Year Plan

Periods. As a result, alternative curriculum and teaching-learning materials were evolved. These steps provided an opportunity to the children for attending NFE centres to move forward to continue their educational pursuits either through formal channel or middle level NFE programme.

The States did not have much experience with regard to effective implementation of middle level NFE programme. This called for development of guidelines for formulating a curriculum frame and instructional package for the middle level NFE programme.

5.4.7. Growth of Upper Primary NFE Programme

The department has developed guidelines for the development of a training manual for the second i.e. middle level NFE programme. The discussions in the workshop helped the department in reviewing the past experiences and building-up a new set of guidelines for curriculum development at this stage. The training material provides concrete suggestions about the objectives, conceptual contexts, methodologies, weightages of different subjects,design of training schedules, etc. It also contain's detailed daily schedule of activities as well as weekly plan of activities.

5.4.8. Availability of Teaching Materials in Tribal Dialect

One of the important barriers to learning for the tribal children is the dearth of materials in tribal dialects. The participation in the teaching-learning process and academic achievement of the tribal children remain low due to a communication gap between the learners and the material. In order to help the States in this crucial task, the department launched a number of programmes for the development of teaching-learning materials and supplementary reading materials in major tribal dialects using regional/state language scripts.

In this endeavour, the department actively sought the collaboration of Central Institute of Indian Languages, Mysore, Tribal Research Institute, Hyderabad, Tribal Research Institute, Ranchi various University Departments, SCERTs and Literacy House, Lucknow.

5.4.9. Problems before Teachers of Tribal Areas

One of the problems faced by the non-tribal teachers is the lack of exposure to the cultural life of various tribal communities and their inability to communicate fluently in the tribal language. In order to extend academic help to the States for equipping the teachers working in tribal areas in effectively implementing NFE programme at the primary level, the department developed an outline of training package for the tribal teacher leaders and teachers working in tribal areas. This will help the functionaries working in tribal areas to organise a variety of teaching-learning activities according to the teaching-learning situations obtainable in the tribal belts. The training package which is under preparation has now been transferred to a newly constituted sister department.

5.4.10. Materials for Educating SC Children

For providing educational facilities for the promotion of education and providing social safe-guards for children belonging to scheduled caste communities, the government of India has a number of schemes. It is essential for functionaries working with children from scheduled caste communities to know about these various schemes and constitutional provisions so that they can acquaint the children about these. It is expected that such knowledge and understanding about the schemes and constitutional provisions will develop awareness among them about these available facilities. This will help in enhancing the participation level of the children from this community in the educational process.

5.4.11. Educational Uplift of Scheduled Caste Communities

The scheduled caste community is economically and educationally every backward in India. In order to create a demand for education among scheduled caste children, the department developed two types of resource materials. The first type of materials was in the form of bibliographical reading materials on eminent scheduled caste persons. The first book in the series was titled Dr. B.R. Ambedkar's thoughts on Education. The second type was on educational developments of scheduled caste communities.

5.4.12. Resource Development in States and Voluntary Organisations

As a National Resource Centre for NFE, the department mounted a series of programmes and activities at the States and voluntary organisation levels. The main focus of these programmes and activities were to generate a sound technical resource base and building up capabilities at the state and voluntary organisation levels.

The department also organised every year four regional level training programmes specially designed to address the problems and issues faced by the voluntary organisations receiving grants from Ministry of Human Resource Development. The training programmes also helped in joint planning of activities, exchange of experiences in innovative programmes and activities. Through these programmes, the department provided opportunities to the functionaries to develop insights into the learners' learning difficulties and identify the ingredients of effective transactional process. Further the programmes helped the functionaries to understand the approaches and orientation of the NFE teaching-learning materials. As a part of practical training in analysing the instructional package, the functionaries were assigned the task of lesson-wise book analysis. The demonstration lessons and the critical analysis of the lessons in the real live centres concretised the approaches and methodologies of NFE process.

5.4.13. Innovative Methodologies in NFE

The department has designated five leading voluntary organisations located in four regions of the country as its field stations. These are being used for experimentation, innovations of methodologies and trying-out its evaluation tools and teaching-learning materials. These organisations have distinguished themselves through their grassroots level innovations. The Organisations identified are:

i) Rayala Seema Seva Samiti
ii) Samanvya Ashram
iii) Mitraniketan
iv) Loka Shiksha Parishad, R.K.Mission
v) Gandhividya Mandir

These organisations provide real life laboratory situations where the department mounts many of its experimental programmes related to teaching-learning material, development programmes and identification of potential learner specific teaching-learning strategies.

The department has also intensively tried-out its MLL based material series in Janakalyan Ashram, Sahajahanpur (U.P.), Lokajumbish (Rajasthan), Konark Education Soceity (New Delhi) and Prayas (New Delhi).

5.5. Extension Activities

5.5.1. Extension of Activities

Except educating the poor and school drop outs, the department also involve in a number of other activities. The important among them are its role as a National Resource Centre for NFE. In order to provide a forum for sharing of experiences among states and voluntary organisations on crucial issues related to NFE programme implementation the department holds a National Conference in NFE each year. It is a forum in which the policy makers, and practitioners identify the status of NFE in various states and voluntary organisations. The delegates reflect on the newer developments and strategies evolved in different organisations. There are also open dialogues with regard to the gap areas that would need special attention.

5.5.2. Alternative Schooling

Alternative schooling is another extensional activity of the department. DPEP interventions have enhanced the role of NFE for providing alternative educational strategies through NFE programmes. In this context, the department organised, in collaboration with MHRD, a National Workshop on the issues pertaining to Alternative Schooling strategies at the primary level. The deliberations of the national workshop facilitated in identifying some of the alternative strategies for providing educational facilities to various learner groups.

The national level conferences and national workshops have served as useful forums for generating new ideas and critically examining the crucial issues related to education of non-enrolled and drop-out children faced by different States and UTs. These also helped the MHRD in reviewing and renewing the NFE scheme in response to the changing situations.

5.6. Evaluation

5.6.1. Pupil Evaluation

Evaluation helps to know the effectiveness of the programme. Pupil evaluation is one of the critical areas of concern for the states/UTs. The issue relates to strengthening of evaluation process and strategies for helping the children in the attainment of desirable set of competencies at the completion of primary education. In this context the department engaged itself to the task of re-organisation of MLLs in terms of four semesters of NFE. It also developed outlines of a manual on pupil evaluation strategies, tools and processes. To help the states/UTs in this regard, the department prepared entry level tests and a battery of tests for evaluating the progress of learners at the terminal stage.

5.6.2. Evaluation of Activities of Voluntary Agencies

The success of NFE depends on the efficiency of machineries, which are undertaken the project. The department coordinated the activities related to evaluation of programmes and activities of voluntary organisations in the task of implementation of centrally sponsored NFE scheme. This was done with the help of members of the joint evaluation team. Moreover the pre-sanction appraisal programme for appraising NGOs seeking MHRD grants for NFE programme was also done by the department with assistance from the field advisers of respective states.

5.7. Future Strategy

With an objective to give education to all, the various state governments launched the District Primary Education (DPEP) programme. The main roles of DPEP are:

i) Identification of District and State Level Resource Persons for Non-Formal Education

ii) Training of District and State level Resource Teams

iii) Continuous technical and academic support for the district and state level teams

iv) Creation of relevant curriculum frame, guidelines and proto- type materials for various groups of learners

The department, through its field research based programmes and activities plans to identify and address the crucial areas of concern connected with learning difficulties of learners attending different educational programmes. These activities will provide sound basis for evolving strategies for training of functionaries working in different alternative schooling models at the Primary school stage.

The cardinal principles for planning intervention strategies will be strengthening academic support to the States and Voluntary Organisations for resource generation and capability building at the grassroot level. The core teams at the state and district levels will be equipped in a way to meet the challenges of education for all through alternative schooling modalities. In this endeavour the States and Voluntary Organisations will be helped to strengthen mutual support system.

5.8. Conclusion

India has always given priority to educate the common man. For this objective, the country has introduced a number of programmes to raise the literacy rate. Still, such projects are going on. Poor percapita income and poverty forced a large number of people to discontinue education. The number of child labourers is also high. Now, the country is trying to reduce the number of drop outs by giving food and free education to the children.

References

Aggarwal, J.C., *Progress of Education in Free India: Modern Indian Education and its problems*, Arya, New Delhi, 1977.

Barnahas, A.P., *Caste in Chanding India: The Indian Institute of Public Administration*, New Delhi, 1965.

Caron, G and Carr-Hill, R.A., *Non-formal education: information and planning issues*, International Institute for Educational Planning, Paris, 1991.

Coombs, Prosser, R.C and Ahmed, H., *New Paths to learning for rural children and youth*, ICED, New York, 1973.

Dodds, T., "The use of distance in non-formal education", The Commonwealth of Learning and the International Extension College, Cambridge, 1996.

Edger Faure, et al., "Learning to Be, A World of Education Today and Tomorrow", *UNESCO*, Paris, 1972.

Galanter Marc, *Competing Equalities: Law and the Backward Classes in India*, Oxford, New Delhi, 1984.

Government of India, *First Backward Classes Commission Report*, New Delhi, 1953.

Herdero, J.M., *Rural Development and social change: An Experiment in Non-Formal Education*, Monohar, Delhi 1977.

6

Status of Literacy in India

6.1. Introduction

Literacy is the minimum requirement to lead a decent life and it is the yardstick of development. A person who can merely read but cannot write is not classified as literate. Any formal education or minimum educational standard is not necessary to be considered literate.

The problems of illiteracy are not confined to India, but are also a malady in developed countries too. Poverty and illiteracy go hand in hand, the poor are disenfranchised, cut off from the democratic process. Any account that does not discuss the political interests served by allowing a large proportion of the American people to remain disenfranchised does not touch the heart of the matter. Before the Civil War in the United States, it was illegal to teach slaves to read, for reading was acknowledged, as the tool needed to understand the social, historical, behavioural and physical laws that control the human condition.

An apprehension of those forces invests human beings with the capacity to alter the conditions of their lives. It is not too far fetched to draw an analogy between slaves in the nineteenth century and illiterate Americans today. Achieving a literate society in which adults can fully participate in the workplace, community, and family will be a major challenge for the world in the coming millennium.

Illiteracy is one of the major problems faced by the developing world, specially Africa and South-East Asia and has been identified as the major cause of socio-economic and ethnic conflicts that frequently surface in the region.

6.2. Importance of Literacy

Human beings are social animals. Education teaches them how to behave in a society. Without education, we all degrade as animals. We calculate all the pros and cons before doing something. Education empower us take a good decision in our life and it segregate our life from wrong. So, education is inevitable for nation building process.

With this outlook in mind, India takes necessary steps to give education to all. Mass literacy programme is one among them. The focus of mass literacy efforts is in terms of basics—the mechanics of reading and attention to computation (addition, subtraction, multiplication and division) in mathematics. It is recognised that these basics are not rooted in the goals of higher-order thinking—conceptualising, inferring, inventing, testing, hypothesis and thinking critically. It is true that these literacy programmes do not have in mind, literacy practice that would promote capacities for independent reasoning, of the kind sought by Third World socially minded pedagogues.

A candid analysis of illiteracy's political and cultural consequences throughout the population will necessitate in our seeking to move literacy expectations beyond a rudimentary ability to read, write and calculate. The recognition that 'literacy' has to be situationally relevant has given rise to the concept of 'functional literacy', which has been referred to by the Second Education Commission.

The need to go into the broader aspect is for the purpose of determining the structure of the system. In devising the system, educational and psychological philosophies of Adler, Dewey, Witttgenstein, Chomsky and our own Mahatma Gandhi and other experiences will come into play. Indeed, it is probably in recognition of this limited scope of literacy, that our constitution makes a reference to education and educational opportunities and not to literacy.

6.2.1. Literacy and Human Rights

Every individual has the right to education. It must be free, at least in the elementary and fundamental stages. But unfortunately, the number of children who are thrown out of formal education is increasing. It has changed as the business of the wealthy. Moreover, education has changed into a profit making business.

Education promotes general culture, abilities, judgment and sense of responsibility to become a useful member of society and opportunity to recreation, and play to attain the same purpose as of education. But the number of students who go for higher education is also decreasing. Now, it is needed a huge amount of money for fulfilling the ambitions in education.

6.2.2. Literacy and Human Development

Education has an important role in a nation's development. It uplifts the standard of living. Investment potential on human capital has now been recognised. The main component of a country's productive wealth is physical assets. But according to World Bank's assessment for 192 countries, physical capital on average accounts only for 16% of total wealth. More important is natural wealth, which accounts for 20%. And more important still is human capital, which accounts for 64%. Literacy is now part of the Human Development Index.

By improving people's ability to acquire and use information, education deepens their understanding of themselves and the world, enriches their minds by broadening their experiences, and improves the choices they make as consumers, producers and citizens. Education strengthens their ability to meet their wants and those of their family by increasing their productivity and their potential to achieve a higher standard of living. By improving people's confidence and their ability to create and innovate, it multiplies their opportunities for personal and social achievement. Japan's rapid industrialisation after the Meiji Restoration was fuelled by its aggressive accumulation of technical skills, which in turn was based on the already high level of literacy and a strong commitment to education, especially the training of engineers.

Literacy holds an important place as a parameter to measure development in the field of development economics. The "Human Development Index" (HDI) developed by UN is a measure of the overall development of the country. One of the three components used in the calculation of HDI is "literacy" as it is a cumulative measure of several factors that contribute to human development.

Literacy is a basic element of a nationwide knowledge system. The most important element of a literacy programme is not the programme itself, but the incentive to become and remain literate. When people are able to believe that they can improve their lives through their own efforts, when they realise that some newly created opportunity is denied to them by illiteracy, then they will learn how to read, write and count.

Development is not simply economic development. It also depends on the physical and mental development of a person. Education takes the responsibility of a person's overall development. Education is the birth right all human beings. It is essential for individual development and fulfilment. The capacity of an individual to contribute to societal development is made possible and enhanced by his or her development as an individual. In this light, education is also a basic need. It is also a means by which other needs, both collective and individual, are realised. Education is the instrument by which the skills and productive capacities are developed and endowed. All these interrelationships of education and development are inseparable from the conception of educational policies.

The problems of illiteracy will not solve by itself in the flux of time. Without organised literacy action, illiteracy will continue to stagnate indefinitely along with the associated ills of poverty and underdevelopment. Experience has shown that determined literacy action is the exception and that more often, literacy campaigns are 'turned on' and 'turned off' in line with short-term policy changes. Literacy and Education have overlapping connotations both as an engine of socio-economic progress as well as for individual growth.

6.2.3. State-wise Education Aids

To develop an educated generation is the responsibility of the government. The state can implement its progressive activities only through the educated inhabitants. Educational expansion has created the conditions for freer individual expression, for a more active participation in the body politic, for what particles called "sound judges of policy," and for greater respect for human welfare and dignity. Many feel, as indeed the constitution makers felt, that education is its own reward- i.e. the more one is educated, the greater is his possibility of developing these qualities. Thus, they believed that the future and hope of mankind lie in educational advancement and a welfare State has to make suitable provision for the same. Education is valuable by itself for discovering the treasure within.

The state has the major responsibility to spread education. It should, therefore, take upon itself all activities and steps to move towards this goal. A strong case can be made for State intervention in education on two counts, namely, the externality effects of education and the alleged incompetence or ignorance of parents. Advocates of State education in the past have usually rested their case predominantly on the two extra economic considerations of equality of opportunity and social cohesion.

6.3. Constitutional Provisions

6.3.1. Education for Social Change

The Indian Constitution has recognised the significance of education for social transformation. It is a document committed to social justice. The Preamble affirms a determination to secure liberty of thought, expression, belief, faith and worship and equality of status and opportunity and to promote amongst the people a feeling of fraternity, ensuring the dignity of the individual and the unity of the nation. Literacy forms the cornerstone for making the provision of equality of opportunity a reality. The objective specified in the Preamble contains the basic structure of the Constitution, which cannot be amended, and the preamble may be invoked to determine the ambit of Fundamental Rights and Directive Principles of State Policy.

Judicial interpretation has brought alive many an Article of the Constitution, which if read literally may seem to be a colourless Article. In Francis Coralie Mulin v. Administrator, Union Territory of Delhi, Justice Bhagwati observed: "The fundamental right to life which is the most precious human right and which forms the arc of all other rights must therefore be interpreted in a broad and expansive spirit so as to invest it with significance and vitality which may endure for years to come and enhance the dignity of the individual and the worth of the human person. We think that the right to life includes right to live, with human dignity and all that goes along with it, namely, the bare necessaries of life such as adequate nutrition, clothing and shelter and facilities for reading, writing and expressing oneself in diverse forms, freely moving about, mixing and co-mingling with fellow human beings."

6.3.2. Specific Constitutional Provisions

There have been specific amendments to the Constitution affecting education, as can be seen in 42nd, 73rd, 74th and 83rd Amendment Acts. These amendments pertain to provisions to enable education being included in the Concurrent List, devolution of powers to local bodies and making elementary education a Fundamental Right formally (from its present status of Directive Principles though this has been ruled as such through judicial interpretation even otherwise).

6.3.3. Equality of Educational Opportunity

All are equal under law. Indian constitution also ensures equal opportunity to all. Since 'Equality of Opportunity' is a basic feature of the Constitution, judicial interpretation has been sought on the different facets of this principle of equality of educational opportunity. For many, egalitarianism in education is seen as a powerful force for the achievement of a just, more equitable society through its contribution to greater social mobility, the 'breaking of any connection between the distribution of education and distribution of personal income.' Yet the "equality of education" concept can be given a variety of interpretations, each leading to different policy outcomes.

Equality of education may concern equality of access to education, equality of educational treatment or equality of ultimate educational performance. Our courts have wrestled with this problem in the face of affirmative action or what is known as 'positive discrimination' in favour of the deprived sections while at the same time preserving the needs of quality of education and fair play. The criteria used for identifying aptitudes, or 'intelligence' are themselves correlated with the social background. So, the liberal goal of providing education according to each individual's capacity or aptitude is unhelpful.

Hence society must adopt special methods to compensate for the deficiencies of the environment in which children grow and which account largely for their unequal educational performance; this would take the form of a national policy of 'positive discrimination' in favour of the underprivileged. The Constitutional provisions have come in very useful to resolve what are essentially political and ideological objectives and the policy conflict of parental free-choice versus educational equality, to avoid bringing about a marked decline in educational standards.

6.3.4. Litigation and Education

In the field of litigation and education, the huge volume of litigation and the mass of decided cases interpreting constitutional provisions are a sufficient testimony to the usefulness of constitutional provision. The pronouncements of the courts have been on varied subjects, affecting the quality and quantity of educational services not only encompassing service and management equities, but also such academic questions as medium of instruction access and autonomy of institutions. That the government has sought to bring forward amendments also shows its imperative to continue to use this document to pursue this welfare objective. In fact, the sheer load of litigation may be proving a bane in one sense, negating the very purpose for which such constitutional provisions are sought. It has also been lamented that follow-up action on constitutional amendments had either not taken place, or slow in implementation.

6.3.5. Education and Judiciary

The primary function of the Executive and the Legislature is the economic transformation. But where justice is the end product and its content has socio-economic components, the constitution, which is the gist of all power, commands the judges to catalyse and control, monitor and mandate by writs, orders and direction—vide Arts. 32 and 226- so that they may bear true faith and allegiance to the constitution and say that 'thy will shall be done.' The interventions of the judiciary from time to time upholding the responsibilities of the State in the all-important educational endeavours, have been positive in providing directions.

India has always given priority to education and it has also a long tradition of organised education. However, educational effort in the country has come a long way from this traditional position in its definition, coverage as well as impact. The current educational system in the country operates in an altogether different context from the classical past. The country's commitment to the provision of education for all and its endeavour to achieve this goal in a speedy fashion has to be seen in this complex milieu within which the educational system is currently functioning.

India follows a policy of equality of educational opportunities to humanise and strengthen the society. Between 1813 and 1921, the British administrators laid the foundations of the modern educational system. The principal positive contribution of the British administrators to equality was to give all citizens open access to educational institutions maintained from or supported by public funds. For instance, the worst difficulties were perhaps encountered when the problem of educating the "untouchable" castes came up.

India has always given higher priority to education. But during the pre-British period, the Indians keep off some religions from acquiring educating by branding them the untouchables. But when the Britain dominated this land, the Indians realised the importance of spreading education.

The evil of untouchability was so prevalent in India and so the upper class created separate schools for their children. Even though the Indian society has developed a lot, even now, some communities in Indian states are kept away from education.

During British rule, the administrators established, firmly and unequivocally, the right of every child irrespective of caste, sex or traditional taboos, to seek admission to all schools supported or aided by public funds. The British administrators refused to accept the principle of compulsory elementary education. The Indian nationalist thought, however, was firmly of the view that the provision of equality of educational opportunity must include a certain minimum general education to be provided to all children on a free and compulsory basis. A demand that four years of compulsory education should be provided to all children was put forward, for the first time before the Indian Education

Commission by Dadabhai Naoroji in 1881. Gopal Krishna Gokhale who moved a resolution on the subject in the Central Legislative Assembly in 1910 and again took the proposal vide a bill in 1912, neither of which achieved their objective.

Later, the Indian government decided to assist local governments to extend comprehensive systems of education in the several provinces. Each province has its own educational system, which has grown up under local conditions and become familiar to the people as a part of their general well being. In view of the diverse social conditions in India there cannot in practice be one set of regulations and one rate of progress for the whole of India. Even within provinces there is scope for greater variety in types if institutions that exists today.

The government of Indian always encourages local governments' interest and initiative in education. Principles, bearing on education in its wider aspects and under modern conditions and conceptions, on oriental and on the special needs of the domiciled community, were discussed at three important conferences of experts and representative non-officials held within the last two years. These principles are the basis of accepted policy. How far they can at any time find local application must be determined with reference to local conditions.

India witnessed great uproars from the public for compulsory education in the beginning of the 20th century. As a result, between 1918 and 1931 compulsory education laws were passed for most parts of the country by the newly elected State legislatures in which Indians were in majority. In 1937, Mahatma Gandhi put forward his scheme of basic education under which education of seven or eight years duration was to be provided for all children and its content was to be revolutionised by building it round a socially useful productive craft.

As an impact of high demand for education from public, the India conceptualised the idea that it was the duty of the state to provide free and compulsory education to all children till they reached the age of 14 years was nationally accepted as an important aspect of the overall effort to provide equality of opportunity. Under the wise leadership of Sir John Sargent, the then educational adviser to the government of India, these ideas were accepted by the British administrators and the Post-war Plan of educational development in India known popularly as the Sargent Plan, put forward proposals to provide free and compulsory basic education to all children in the age group 6-14 over a period of 40 years.

However, the nationalist opinion rejected this long period, and a committee under the chairmanship of B.G. Kher proposed that this goal could and should be achieved in a period of 16 years. It was this recommendation that was eventually incorporated in the Constitution as a Directive Principle of State Policy. It was thus not a mere statement of an ideal, but a well-thought out enunciation of a policy, which is yet to be implemented though a substantial component was sought to be achieved by 2000 under the education for all plan.

6.4. Education for All

6.4.1. Basic Level

India envisaged providing education for all even if it is very difficult to practice. For this, India gave prime importance to basic level education. Through basic level, India aims to make each and every individual the ability of read and write. While preparing the document education for all, the Ministry of Human Resource Development has brought out a compendium of relevant statistics, culled out from the annual statements regularly sent by the state governments.

A large number of people in India are not able to write even their names. So, the core curriculum is emphasised at the elementary school level. This is a carefully planned curriculum that in content it compares favourably with those adopted in a number of other countries. A common core can help in overcoming discrepancies between the educational opportunities of urban and rural people, and that of men and women, but it cannot eliminate those difficulties unless literacy rates improve, greater participation occurs in school and other changes take place in society.

The success of education programmes depend on:

— Accessibility,

— Availability,

— Quantity,
— Quality,
— Inter-connectivity
— Equity, and
— Utility.

Education has the power to narrow down the gaps between different social groups. As progress in the quantitative expansion of education, this gap is narrowing, but still, inequities within the educational system of the country continue to be quite sharp. Presenting the literacy level of different components of the population brings out the nature of this multi-level system of inequities. But, even after the improved statistics, the pyramidal structure has not undergone any significant change in terms of reduction of inequities in any large measure.

The Government's efforts in the direction of universalisation of elementary education through school system have both its gains and shortcomings. Gains lay in the direction of quantitative expansion, and shortcomings have been in the direction of quality and equity as between different sections of the populace.

6.4.2. Adult Education

Adult illiteracy was the major problem before the government of India since independence and so the eradication of illiteracy has been one of the major national concerns. During the first Five Year Plan, the programme of social education, inclusive of literacy, was introduced as part of the community development programme.

India adopted a number of efforts to irradiate illiteracy. Among these, the Gram Shikshan Mohim initiated in Satara district of Maharashtra in 1959 was one of the successful mass campaigns. It aimed at completing literacy work village-by-village within a short period of 3 to 6 months, through the honorary services of primary teachers and middle-school and high school students, supported by the entire community. It achieved a good deal of success but suffered from the lack of follow-up due to financial constraints and some of its good work was lost as a consequence. In spite of these varied initiatives the programme of adult literacy did not make much headway.

India put forward a national policy on education in 1968 to endorse the recommendations of the education commission as well as for reiterating the significance of universal literacy and developing adult and continuing education as matters of priority. While the formal elementary education programme was supplemented by a non-formal education system, it was also decided to undertake adult literacy programmes culminating in the total literacy mission approach.

Basic literacy, functionality and civic awareness were the three components of the adult education programme. The programme covers different schemes so that finally it aims at helping learners achieve a 'reasonable degree of self-reliance in literacy and functionality and better appreciation of the scope and value of science.

The national leaders of India tried to spread education among adults even before independence. Mahatma Gandhi, the father of Indian nation, was the one among those prominent leaders. Envisaging education for all, Gandhiji conducted many constructive programmes to make districts completely literate.

Gandhiji could succeed in a certain level. The district of Surat, in erstwhile Bombay Presidency had been totally literate, but again relapsed into illiteracy for lack of follow-up. There were efforts at spreading by the Baroda Rulers, supplemented by a live library movement. Here again lack of follow-up and sustained efforts caused a relapse into illiteracy among the vulnerable sections. There were voluntary agencies working in the field. Some agencies as the Karnataka Adult Education Council, Gujarat Social Education Committee and Bombay City Social Education Committee have had large programmes extending to the whole state or a metropolitan city. Literacy House of Lucknow did commendable work in this field.

In the university level, the University Grants Commission considered the general pattern of development and assistance towards adult education. Departments of Continuing Education took up the work of "University goes to Masses." The slogan "Each One, Teach One" caught the imagination of not only the students, but also a large number of educated individuals, and it looked like these programmes will meet a major success. However, like most enthusiastically launched programmes, they also fell by the wayside.

In 1968-69, a farmers training and functional literacy project was launched, coordinating the activities of Ministries of Education, Agriculture and Information & Broadcasting. The Central Advisory Board of Education in its November 1975 meeting asked that the exclusive emphasis on formal system of education should be given up and a large element of non-formal education should be introduced within the system.

The major problem before India in the field of education was the large number of dropouts from the formal education. India is still facing this problem. So, the prominent objective of the non-formal education system was to tackle the problem of dropouts from the formal system. The dropout from the formal system continues to hover around 50% and have not shown any great variation in the last four decades. It is not difficult to guess the collective identities of the victims, children who fail to survive at school. They are children of landless agricultural labourers and subsistence peasants. Caste-wise, a substantial proportion of them belong to the Scheduled Castes that have been granted special rights including reservation in higher education and representative bodies, in the Constitution.

Caste system is the worst villain in education. India has been the grip of casteism and is not ready to tolerate the lower caste people. The situation of children belonging to many of the Scheduled Tribes is worse, especially in the central Indian belt. Forest-dwelling tribal communities have had to bear the brunt of State initiatives in dam construction, development of tourism with the help of game sanctuaries and mining. Apart from such destabilising experiences, bias against tribal cultures and languages also makes the school curriculum and the teacher a deterrent for the advancement of tribal education. There are about 40 million rural artisans in India. For them, the current standard school curriculum is trivial, and in a sense irrelevant and demeaning. No wonder, one realises in a rather simple, unscientific way, these children stop coming to school early.

The children residing in slums, living in conditions of uncertainly and violence is always a likely case of early withdrawal or elimination. In keeping with recent trends in the international literacy movement, the emphasis of mass literacy programmes in India shifted from 'literacy' to 'adult education' through the intermediate phases of 'functional literacy' and 'non-formal education' during the last fifty years. The policy statement of the present programme highlights the development of functional competencies and awareness of the adult learners as two of the three equally important components of the national adult education programme. The third component is obviously literacy. Our universities had also been roped into this activity.

6.4.2.1. National Adult Education Programme (NAEP)

To check the wide spreading illiteracy among adults, India introduced the National Adult Education Programme (NAEP). Literacy is an indispensable component of any nation. A view to provide education to the millions of illiterate persons in the age-group 15-35, this programme was set up. Through NAEP, the government aimed to provide skills for self-directed learning leading to self-reliant and active role in their own development and in the development of their environment.

The basic components of NAEP are the three R's, social awareness and functionality. In spite of careful planning before the launch of this programme, the Sardar Patel Institute of Social and Economic Research, after a survey carried out in the initial flush of enthusiasm, observed about the progress of the programme in a progressive state like Gujarat: "On the whole, while the NAEP in Gujarat was generally found to be addressed to the target groups kept in view under the NAEP and it was found to have some other commendable aspects, all things considered, its achievement in terms of spread of literacy is rather modest, and more so in terms of social awareness and functionality."

6.4.2.2. Literacy Mission (NLM)

To strengthen the adult literacy activities, India later introduced the National Literacy Mission (NLM). During the era of the high profile technology missions, some attention was given to issues like immunisation, safe drinking water and literacy along with talk of people's participation and social audit of these programmes.

In 1989, the district-based Total Literacy Campaigns (TLC) emerged as a programme strategy for the National Literacy

Mission against this background. While it was correctly envisaged that the initial social mobilisation for a time-bound campaign provides the inspiration to spark for a mass participation of people, volunteering their time and energy for a cause like literacy, the follow-up programme was not worked out clearly. However, admitting and recognising the many flaws and failures of the 'campaign approach', even as early as 1994, NLM continued with the same TLC strategy and tried to bolster it with better monitoring, internal evaluation and presently with a revival effort through what is called 'Operation Restoration'.

Though the Total Literacy Campaigns helped in fostering a participatory approach in dealing with this issue, the problem of sustaining the momentum has remained. In the budget for 1999-2000, allocation for the Rural Functional Literacy Project does not find a special mention. The overall allocation to adult education has, however, been increased by about 40%.

Lack of funds and lame pedagogical methods hinder the success of adult education in India. Countries like India which have a long tradition of transmission of ideas and wisdom orally, individual and societal transformations through a mass literacy campaign, are rather a form of renewal in nature than being additive or extensive. There is also the problem continued sustenance of the campaign approach. There are some hopeful signs of ICT-supported services being used to bridge the gulf. Some collaborative partnership of the Government of India and non-governmental agencies in partnership with international organisations and private sector has been mooted and the results of such collaborative efforts may perhaps show a way.

In India, a large number of people enter adulthood without proper education and consequently their self-confidence is shaky. In a fast-changing environment of economic and cultural change, they will continue to be edged out unless their capacities are actively consolidated and improved so as to encounter the world outside on equal terms. This programme can be in the nature of a Sunset programme; but till then, i.e. literacy becomes self-sustaining fact with self-arising demand for its very usefulness and need for a fuller life, no Government should be allowed to ignore this aspect.

Besides spreading literacy, the NLM aims to achieve skill formation, functionality, social awareness, organisation for participation in development. While this indicates a commitment to some kind of holistic approach, and some expectation of link between literacy, education and social development, it also reflects certain assumptions regarding illiteracy, lack of awareness, skills and functionality—which we have contested earlier.

Like any other programme, the NLM also faced some initial hiccups, ie, lack of conceptual clarity, regarding literacy, education, social development and of the complex inter-relationships between them. To a considerable extent, this was an inherited legacy of the 'filtration theory' of education, which viewed eradication of illiteracy as a dependent function of educational development. In today's language of development studies, it was a 'top-down' approach. This has exacerbated an already existing tension which emerges from any programme with finite means and multiple objectives.

It is legitimate to talk of the literate helping the non-literate to become literate, it is not legitimate to talk of the 'educated' helping the 'uneducated' adult to become educated. To be non-literate is not the same as being 'uneducated'. In general, because of the pejorative connotations of the term illiteracy and the sense of disdain it seems to suggest for the people's rich oral traditions and its associated skills, etc., it might not be amiss indeed it may be wiser—to use, wherever possible, the term non-literate rather than illiterate. Since convenience might demand the continued use of the terms illiterate or illiteracy, there should be, at the least, an abiding awareness of what should not be implied in the use of such terms.

The structures of non-formal education in its various forms, from literacy campaigns to centre-based or more flexible vocational training schemes provided by government sponsored institutions or voluntary organisations remain important sources for the dissemination to adults of relevant information/knowledge/skills. But the efficacy of non-formal education is decisively dependent on decentralised and locally relevant strategies for socioeconomic development, planned jointly by local learners, and agencies.

Education is the heart and soul of a society. So, the structures of informal education constitutes the structures of society itself. To demand that they be accessible and responsive to all or to most adults is to demand much greater cultural empowerment and cultural democratisation. This is inseparable from, but not congruent with, the demand for greater political empowerment and political democratisation.

No policy committed to the spread and deepening of education, whether emanating from the NLM, from other government bodies, or from any other quarter, can do other than announce its commitment to the preservation and strengthening of India's democratic and secular polity, though this is not the only reason why any government programme regarding literacy or education must necessarily be part of and integrated and holistic government policy and perspective.

6.5. Strategies to Promote Literacy

It is the duty of the central and state government to spread education. The education system has undergone many types of changes and experiments. Many a new thought and idea has been tried out and implemented at some point of time and in some part of the country. The various departments of education of the universities all over the country have been deliberating over the various facets of the problem and the treatises submitted for the M.Ed. and Ph.D courses are a veritable storehouse of ideas. Then, there are the various centres of advanced studies which can distill the various ideas and have also been rendering advisory services. The number of enquiry commissions, whether it be the Royal Commissions, or Commissions appointed thereafter headed by Indians of eminence, are not insignificant.

Education helps to reduce the gap between haves and have nots even if it is a 'vast, shapeless and vexatious subject.' In a country of continental proportions, with its different communities and people with different socio-economic backgrounds, and literally living in different centuries in terms of thought, the aims of education can be at variance with the thoughts of experts in the field. And even among the latter, there are different perceptions.

Education field faces a lot of chaos. One among them is the burgeoning of new opportunities and aspirations for hundreds of millions who had so long been denied all education and were living at a level of tragic deprivation. Education is the key to help us in the transition process. So, it should value and promote excellence. To support excellence is not to oppose the concept of equality of opportunity.

According to Jean Piaget, "The principal goal of education is to create men who are capable of doing new things, not simply of repeating what other generations have done- men, who are creative, inventive and discoverers. The second goal of education is to form minds, which can be critical, can verify, and not accept everything they are offered. The great danger today is of slogans, collective opinions, and ready-made trends of thought. We have to be able to resist individually, to criticise, to distinguish between what is proven and what is not."

6.5.1. Literacy in Information Technology Era

People give prime importance to education in this era of information technology. Everything is possible in this era and conventional methods of education involving mastering a script, learning words and sentences, etc., are passé now. That has no direct relationship to everyday life such learners, have to give place a learning that is directly relevant to them.

The Education Division of the Tata Consultancy Services claims to have evolved a system where the learners are exposed to a set of words and pictures that have a direct relevance to them. A set of about 500 words or so form the vocabulary, and by repeated exposure of these words and pictures, the learners become familiar with them and learn to recognise them. This knowledge enables them to even read newspapers and magazines and activates an interest in the learner to know more. If necessary, they can then join a formal education programme. Video projections and large computer screens aid such learning process.

6.5.2. Distribution of Educational Funds

Spreading non-formal education needs a huge amount of money. Most of the NGOs are dependent only on government funding for their activities, and funding them for this activity will be only an indirect government support. With large business houses expressing interest in welfare measures, at least in the geographical regions in which they operate, they can be encouraged to contribute to such causes. Local institutions like Panchayats and Gram Sabhas should also be encouaged to take interest in these activities by impressing on them the fact that an educational community is innovative, peace-loving and involved in community affairs.

6.5.3. Problems in Mass Education Programme

Mass education programmes are also not free from obstacles. There is a general consensus about universalisation of elementary education. This issue has to be beyond politics—in fact, the whole basis for access to educational opportunities at all levels has to be a non-party matter and discussion of its aspects should be beyond party politics an cut across party lines. All major political parties have put it high on their agenda. It is also a positive factor that successive governments have expressed their priority for education. This has now been made an important component of National Human Development Initiative (NHDI) and also the Prime Minister's Special Action Plan. In a situation when the need for strong political commitment is being increasingly felt, these proclaimed intentions of the government are certainly welcome, and help to keep the momentum alive.

Education has had a strong and consistent political commitment in the state and so, the tangible achievements it can mark, is indeed remarkable. As far back as 1819, the ruler of Travancore in south Kerala called for the state to meet the cost of education. Facilities were provided for everyone to have access to education either free or at a small nominal cost. The State continued to make progress and Universal Literacy was achieved in 1991. The State continues to top the literacy chart even in the Census 2001. The case is cited to indicate the importance of enlightened leadership with progressive views to achieve goals.

6.5.4. Education: A Birth Right

Every individual has a right for education. Education is a value in itself and is the bedrock on which any edifice of equality of opportunity can be erected. It opens the road to progress and literacy is a measure of human development. It is easier to plan for sound economic development and a stable political system in an educated society. There is, therefore, every reason to canvass for Right to Education being incorporated as a Fundamental Right.

The histories of our developments in many fields have to be properly projected. But this should not take away the requirements of discipline involved in the learning process. What is required is ensuring irreversibility and giving a sense of perspective by not distorting history. Planning the contents of curriculum for the young mind that gets easily swayed by 'what is taught' rather than 'what is desirable to teach,' is probably more difficult. The commitment of the various political parties on universalisation of elementary education must also converge into a consensus on content and dissemination.

6.6. Community Support to Spread Education

Education is the minimum requirement of development and without education, a nation or a society or a community will not develop. In the system of central planning, only the resources required from the government or public sector agencies are taken into account. However, for an activity like education, there are considerable costs borne by the children and parents. These costs are not included in the financial implications presented, except for the provision of incentives like books and uniforms to the weaker sections.

The Constitution has directed that education for children in primary and upper primary levels of education should be free. This has been so far taken in practice, to mean that schools should not charge any fees. The cost incurred by parents for education of their children has been ignored and has not been considered as a violation of the directive of free education. In view of the paucity of resources, it may be pragmatic to continue this approach and let the parents bear costs of this nature, while underscoring that ideally these costs should be borne by public funds.

Safeguarding democracy and strengthening the foundations of the integrity is the responsibility of a nation. For upholding these values, a nation should not compromise with the requirements of these basic needs in education. It should be noted that without adequate resources, financial, physical and human, our target of Education For All will remain unachieved even by the turn of the century. If we have to enter the twenty-first century without the burden of the unfulfilled goals originally proposed by the Constitution makers of India, substantial resources should be allocated to elementary and adult education programmes.

6.7. Education, Literacy, Social Development

Education is the corner stone of development of a nation. An understanding of the fundamental terms—education, literacy, social development- and of their inter-relationships, necessarily shape one's perspectives and therefore the policies made or recommended. This understanding in the judgment of the group thus constitutes the basic prism through which the mass literacy campaigns/programme of the NLM will have to be assessed and evaluated.

Education is the means for getting a decent life. It has an important functional or instrumental or utilitarian dimension. The purpose of education is to acquire qualifications for employment/ upward mobility', 'wider/higher (in terms of income) opportunities', 'to meet the needs for trained manpower in diverse fields for national development. But in its deepest sense education is not instrumental. That is to say, it is not to be justified outside of itself.

Education is not a commodity to be acquired or possessed. But it is a process of inestimable importance to individuals and society, although it can and does have enormous use value. Education then, is a process of expansion and conversion, not in the sense of converting or turning out students into doctors, engineers, etc but the widening and turning out of the mind—the creation, sustenance and development of self-critical awareness and independence of thought. It is an inner process of moral-intellectual development. Education is not so much a 'preparation for life' but in the final analysis the finding of a way of life.

Education is the process of acquiring knowledge. Adults may lack training, they do not lack education as they have learnt from life's experiences. Conversely, those who are highly trained are not necessarily highly educated or even reasonably educated. This is not to underrate the importance of skill formation in a developing society, but to put it in proper perspective. The critical difference lies in the learning process—the desire, the capacity, the opportunity.

Skills have to be learnt, but they may be acquired, and practiced through habit without applying any thought or exercising one's judgment. Training in skills which stimulate observation, curiosity and assessment—of its implications, for one's self/others/the environment—is certainly an important component of education. It is in this last sense that we reiterate that adult illiteracy should not be confused with lack of education or training. Adults do not become what they are without learning many things functional and related skills or languages to communicate values, a sense of their own identity, responsibilities, knowledge about their own environment, traditions, culture, and specialised knowledge derived from their occupations, passed on across generations, and added to by their own observations.

Literacy is an empowering skill which reduces many fears, of being lost, cheated, manipulated by others. It also increases access to many types of information that one needs/wants to achieve a more satisfying life, to carry out one's responsibilities more efficiently/effectively, even to challenge/reject, if necessary what has been learnt through one's socialisation in an unequal society. It thus provides for a better life politically, culturally socially and economically.

Education also leads to social development. Social development is different from that of economic and socioeconomic development. Socioeconomic development can be understood for our purposes here as a socially humane and equitable form of economic development. Social development is a wider concept encompassing the latter two terms. It is akin to the striving for "the good society," for which the learning process, of constant enrichment of that process, is an essential and integral element, along with effective, responsible and willing participation and the achievement of a more equitable order.

A better society or better social development leads to better education which leads to better social development, and further improvement of educational opportunities and quality, which in turn improves the prospect of better social development, etc.

A minimum level, and equitable distribution of socioeconomic development is necessary to eradicate hunger, chronic poverty, under- nourishment, malnourishment, permanent indebtedness—which fuel exploitation, powerlessness, dependency and inequality. There must also be access to basic health care and security/shelter i.e. the minimum conditions for decent physical existence must be established for this qualitative leap in the educational-social development spiral to take off.

India aims to achieve complete literacy. Education itself has to play a far more active, participatory and dynamic role, to provide the motive, the rationale, the skills, the values and the vision of what is meant by a better society. At the moment, India is still very far from approaching that level of social development. The inadequacies, inequities and maladies of the educational process are both a cause and effect of this situation.

The relationship between literacy and social development is mediated by the role, spread and quality of education. The problem of adequate socioeconomic development has both an individual and a collective/ social dimension, being a problem not only for the individual but also for society as a whole. Greater literacy in some cases may mean greater/ better opportunities for socio-economic improvement in individual lives/families, without much impact on other factors. Mass poverty, especially, cannot be resolved by treating it as a sum of individual problems to be resolved individually. It must be seen as a collective problem requiring collective solutions.

Because of the criticality of its size and pressure, mass literacy may set off certain chain reactions, on the socioeconomic, and political—administrative structures, the evidence of which we found in many areas. But it cannot by itself resolve the collective problem of mass-scale impoverishment or widening inequalities in socioeconomic conditions. In the absence of collective solutions of these problems, it is extremely difficult to either stabilise newly acquired literacy skills, or set off the spiral movement for social development.

Literacy is a training or skill whose purpose and value is contingent upon the availability of opportunities for its use, and upon benefits, economic, politico-social and cultural, to be derived from its use. The functionality dimension of literacy in India remains a problematic area. Almost as serious a problem as the lack of widespread literacy is the fragility of literacy achievements and the phenomenon of re-lapse of former neo-literates.

6.8. Future Plans

The society is changing so is the field of education. Changing needs of educational technology and entry of computers and integration of information and communication technology demand new structures, which the system should be able to assimilate. Renewal of education also calls for provision for regular reviews, which reckons also changing scenarios and developments in emerging technologies.

Education continuously renews itself in order to prepare for a future rather than for obsolescence. This renewal process derives from a variety of sources which include: the growth of human knowledge, which is the basic component of education; the heritage of collective experience and values which education transmits to the new generations; the means and methods of communication by which knowledge and values are transmitted and the new values and aspirations which the human spirit adds to the collective experience and wisdom of the past or by which the heritage of the past is reinterpreted and reassessed.

6.8.1. Changes in Knowledge Acquiring Process

With the development of society, new theories are also coming into being. In olden days, people believed that the educated people are teaching the illiterate. But the modern theory tells that nobody teaches any one, but men learn from each other. In other words, all are learners. The aim of education is not to fit people into a system but to help them develop their human powers. The new developments in the field of learning have been due to the significant and path-breaking contributions by many scientists.

The shift in emphasis can be seen from coping behaviour to expressive behaviour or from prescriptive behaviour to liberating behaviour or from direct influence to indirect influence. There are three distinct global developments that may affect future of education:

6.8.1.1 Knowledge Growth

The knowledge also develops with the development of science and technology. In the period 600 BC to AD 1700, the body of scientific knowledge doubled every 1000 years; from the beginning of industrialisation until the early twentieth century, the doubling period accelerated to about 200 years; and now in many scientific fields, knowledge is doubling every 15 years or so. Moreover, the lag between a discovery in a fundamental science and its technological application has narrowed remarkably. This enormous growth in the volume and application of knowledge impacts on every aspect of modern life. Parallel to the rapid growth of knowledge is the increasing velocity with which knowledge is being circulated.

New configurations in the fields of knowledge are emerging and are tending to efface to some extent at least, the old established demarcation lines between the natural sciences and the social and human sciences. Cross over points are emerging between the major fields of human activity. Another direction of advance is the aggregation of different components of traditional disciplines into new integrated fields. The most practical conclusion that we draw on education planning is, therefore, that the options open to learners in regard to fields of study should not be closed too early.

6.8.1.2. Education and Communication

The world witnessed an explosion in the field of communication with the development of technology. The communication technologies have multiplied and became more and more powerful. The development in computer technology has affected every individual. Telecommunications and data processing have already increased dramatically the volume of information readily available as well as its accessibility. Integration of information and communication technologies is a new challenge before the educational administrators.

6.8.1.3. Education and Culture

Cultural heritage reflected in the whole range of expressions is the other source of educational renewal. This gives meaning and worth to the society's being. The need for a reaffirmation of cultural identity is more urgent today because of the tendency towards uniformity and homogeneity generated by economic and material forces and the mass media. Next only to the family, the school is the most important institution for the transmission of cultural values. Role of education, an indispensable role, is to be a medium in which the various new influences are assimilated in the cultural stream.

Education has a vital role in promoting the processes by which scientific and technological knowledge is assimilated in the fabric of national life without detriment to the people's values. There is a 'cultural' dimension in every subject taught in the schools. This needs to be brought out in the methods of instruction.

Technological advancements can also be seen in the field of tools and techniques available for pedagogy and androgogy. Educational Technology is the new addition to the armamentarium of pedagogy in the future. The phrase 'Educational Technology' was defined by the National Council of Educational Technology (UK) as the development, application, evaluation of systems, techniques and aids to improve the process of human learning. It has a wider connotation than simply the use of electromechanical and other aids in teaching. It places as much stress on educational ideas as on educational inventions. It can only be of value if it is really integrated into the entire system.

In educational technology, there are two approaches—hardware and software. The hardware approach is based on the application of engineering principles for developing electromechanical equipment like motion pictures, tape recorders, teaching machines, computers, videotape, closed circuit television, etc. The second approach, i.e. software approach uses the principle of psychology for behavior modification purposes. There are two trends or directions of educational technology: towards mass instructional technology and towards technology designed for individual instruction. Mass transmission technology capable of making educational messages is available to millions of children and adults. Television is the most obvious example of mass instructional technology. Teaching machines are examples of individual instructional technology.

6.8.2. Distance learning

This is a method of acquiring education from a distant institute. Distance learning, an aspect of use of Educational Technology, can thus transform traditional learning. Learning at one's own pace and at his convenience will get stressed. Attending formal classroom instruction puts severe stress both on the learner and the society. The former has to schedule his activities in the structured requirements of a formal classroom, which for a person already working may be difficult. The latter has to grapple with difficult-to-find resources to provide for the escalating costs of education. Distance education overcomes these hurdles. Use of satellites is rapidly changing the concept of conventional education. Students need no longer be limited by lack of access, shortage of teachers or interference from work.

6.8.3. Computers

Computers have made a tremendous change in the field of education. It has caused a paradigm shift in the field of technology so much so that we cannot afford to be left out of computer literacy in any future plans for education. With computers, the technological revolution can be stated to have come into the classroom. Technology is an enabling tool. It facilitates the process of writing so that students and teachers alike can interact with the text in useful ways that are difficult with paper and pencil.

6.8.4. Integration of Information and Communication Technologies

Integration of Information and Communication Technologies (ICT) with school needs serious consideration. Teachers, educators, curriculum developers, evaluators and others will have to redefine their roles to tackle ICT rich environment and harness its full potential for the benefit of learners. Information media are bringing about dramatic changes and are facilitating the communication of information between instructor and learner. These media have also produced a basic easing of spatio-temporal limitations and creation of new learning spaces based on information networks. These may call for structural changes. Our politico-administrative structures should be interpreted flexibly enough not to obstruct these winds of change.

6.9. Conclusion

The level of literacy and economic development of a nation is interrelated. A country is having higher literacy rate means it is enjoying high growth rate. To attain development, today, many developing countries are giving priority to education. India is also implementing myriad of education programmes to improve human knowledge. In India, education is the birth right of every citizen. But acute poverty forces the common man to keep off from the process of education. For them, the government is giving continuing education programmes.

References

Basu, A.N., *Education in Modern India,* Orient Book Co., Calcutta, 1947.

Dayal, Bhagwan, *The Development of Modern Indian Education,* Orient Longman, Bombay, 1955.

Gore, M.S., *Indian Education: Structure and Process,* Rawat Publication, Jaipur, 1995.

Gosal, G. S., "Literacy in India: An Interpretative Study", *Rural Sociology,* 1964.

Jolly, K.G., *Literacy for All by 2001: Strategies at District Level,* D.K. Publishers, New Delhi, 1992.

Limaye, P.M., *Education in India Today,* Deccan Education Society, Poona, 1945.

Naik, J.P., *Elementary Education in India: A Promise to keep,* Allied Publishers, Bombay, 1975.

Sharma Amita, Gopal Krishnan R., *A New Strategy for the Total Literacy Campaign,* Document 5, Rajiv Gandhi Mission, June 1999.

7

Adult Education and Approaches to Learning

7.1. Introduction

Educated people are an asset of a nation. So, the primary objective of a government is to educate its people. But unfortunately, all people are not lucky to get a formal education. For them, the government is introducing non-formal education programmes. Adult education, apart of non-formal education, is instructional and related support services for adults who are not enrolled in secondary school; who lack the educational foundation expected of a high school graduate; and whose inability to speak, read, and/or write the English language effectively impairs their ability to function on the job, in their family, and/or in their society. To achieve their goals and develop their knowledge and potential, they are in need of programs to help raise their level of education and self-sufficiency.

7.2. Objectives of Adult Education

Education is a process of acquiring knowledge. Every people learn new things and information in their life. People continue education due to:

7.2.1. Personal Growth and Development

Education is the yardstick of getting a nice job. Unemployment is the curse of any nation and education helps overcome it. According to psychological theories people seek individual self-actualisation and wish to promote individual growth. Someone might join a course or educational programme for the content but also for contact with other people in an agreeable setting.

7.2.2. Social Improvement

Individuals form society and when the life of each individual develops, it leads to the development of society itself. Education helps to attain new knowledge and skills and it will ultimately improve personal or career life. The emphasis is placed on the individual within a larger social context. Thus, someone who left school early might want to get a certificate to show basic competency for employment.

7.2.3. Organisational Effectiveness

This happens when an employer or another type of organisation (e.g., community group, charity, etc) sponsors learning activities so that members, employees, volunteers, etc can reach organisational goals. Sometimes these can be organised through on-site human resource development programs, or individuals and groups of employees might do educational programmes through distance education.

7.2.4. Intellectual Growth

Education stimulates the thinking capacity and it leads to intellectual growth. Many people value learning for its own sake.

7.2.5. Social Transformation

All individuals in a society are leading a decent life, it is the development of that society itself. Education has a major role in the development of a society. Organisations supporting policy advocacy and social change may wish to reach members through education which changes people and challenges existing social systems.

7.3. Doctrines of Adult Education

Illiteracy is a curse and it creates a lot of problems in the life of every individual. People attain education because of various reasons. Whatever mixture of reasons may motivate someone to pursue education and training, effective programmes must be directed at adults in a manner that will be useful to their needs and interests. If they are disappointed, they will stop attending. Effective adult education programmes:

— are based on the needs of the participants and make use of their different experiences,
— seek the participation of individual adults, groups and communities in decision-making at all levels of the learning process; including determination of needs, curriculum development, program implementation and evaluation,
— use course activities that are practical and problem centered,
— engage participants in the learning process through an interactive approach,
— incorporate learners' goals in the activities,
— use discussion and group activities to help create a supportive educational environment,
— demonstrate practical applications of the skills and knowledge gained,
— use logic and sequence of class activities should reinforce lessons learned,
— demonstrate how the material and concepts learned fit together as a package,
— allow for self-appraisal opportunities, use of skills learned, and evaluation/feedback to the instructor.

The government is adopting a lot of education programmes to spread the education among the adults. Examples of Adult Education programmes are:

— Adult basic education,
— Literacy programmes,
— Adult secondary education,
— Life-coping skills,
— Parenting skills,
— Citizenship training for immigrants,
— English as a second language,
— Job-seeking skills,
— Classes for public assistance recipients to prepare them for employment.

7.4. Factors Involved in Adult Learning

India has always given importance to education. After independence, India has started a number of programmes for educating its people. Adult learning is compulsory learning. It is a life long method of acquiring knowledge. Formal college education; job related training, community education, or self improvement, etc are coming under adult learning. It is vital in today's changing world where the facts and approaches we learned in our formal education are obsolete within a few years. Life-long learning has visible economic implications, contributes to the growth of society, helps bring about change, and improves the quality of life for the individual.

Adult learning is all about change - change in attitude, change in knowledge, change in behaviour, change in a skill, change in how we think, and change in productivity. It is a major component of lifelong learning, the third pillar alongside school education and higher education. Adult education has a wide meaning. First of all, it aims to educate the adults. Adult learning encompasses learning for personal, civic and social purposes as well as for employment-related purposes. It takes place in a variety of environments in and outside the formal education and training systems.

Adult learning is inherently joyful, that adults are innately self-directed learners, that good educational practice always meets the needs articulated by learners themselves and that there is a uniquely adult learning process as well as a uniquely adult form of practice. The attempt to construct an exclusive theory of adult learning - one that is distinguished wholly by its standing in contradiction to what we know about learning at other stages in the lifespan - is a grave error. Indeed, a strong case can be made that as we examine learning across the lifespan the variables of culture, ethnicity, personality and political ethos assume far greater significance in explaining how learning occurs and is experienced than does the variable of chronological age.

7.4.1. Self-Directed Learning

When we become adults, we ourselves take decisions. In the same way, self-directed learning focuses on the process by which adults take control of their own learning, in particular how they set their own learning goals, locate appropriate resources, decide on which learning methods to use and evaluate their progress. Work on self-direction is now so widespread that it justifies an annual international symposium devoted solely to research and theory in the area.

There are a lot of factors affect the learning capacity of an adult. They are the adult's previous experiences, the nature of the learning task and domain involved, the political ethos of the time - affect the decision to learn in this manner. A view of learning which views adults as self-contained, volitional beings scurrying around engaged in individual projects is one that works against cooperative and collective impulses. Citing self-direction, adults can deny the importance of collective action, common interests and their basic interdependence in favour of an obsessive focus on the self.

7.4.2. Critical Reflection

Adults are capable of this kind of learning can be found in developmental psychology, where a host of constructs such as embedded logic, dialectical thinking, working intelligence, reflective judgment, post-formal reasoning and epistemic cognition describe how adults come to think contextually and critically. As an idea critical reflection focuses on three interrelated processes;

a) The process by which adults question and then replace or reframe an assumption that up to that point has been uncritically accepted as representing commonsense wisdom,

b) The process through which adults take alternative perspective on previously taken for granted ideas, actions, forms of reasoning and ideologies, and

c) The process by which adults come to recognise the hegemonic aspects of dominant cultural values and to understand how self-evident renderings of the 'natural' state of the world actually bolster the power and self-interest of unrepresentative minorities.

Many tasks remain for researchers of critical reflection as a dimension of adult learning. A language needs to be found to describe this process to educators which is more accessible than the psychoanalytic and critical theory terminology currently employed. More understanding of how people experience episodes of critical reflection, and how they deal with the risks of committing cultural suicide these entail, would help educators respond to fluctuating rhythms of denial and depression in learners. Much research in this area confirms that critical reflection is context or domain-specific.

Theoretical analyses of critical reflection considerably outweigh the number of ethnographic, phenomenological studies of how this process is experienced. Contextual factors surrounding the decision to forgo or pursue action after a period of critical reflection are still unclear, as is the extent to which critical reflection is associated with certain personality characteristics.

7.4.3. Experiential Learning

Experience is the best teacher. It is central to the concept of andragogy. Adult teaching should be grounded in adults' experiences, and that these experiences represent a valuable resource, is currently cited as crucial by adult educators of every conceivable ideological hue. The adult education practice affirms the importance of experiential methods such as games, simulations, case studies, psychodrama, role play and internships and many universities now grant credit for adults' experiential learning. Not surprisingly, then, the gradual accumulation of experience across the contexts of life is often argued as the chief difference between learning in adulthood and learning at earlier stages in the lifespan. Yet, an exclusive reliance on accumulated experience as the defining characteristic of adult learning contains two discernible pitfalls.

Experience should not be thought of as an objectively neutral phenomenon, a river of thoughts, perceptions and sensations into which we decide, occasionally, to dip our toes. Rather, our experience is culturally framed and shaped. How we experience events and the readings we make of these are problematic; that is, they change according to the language and categories of analysis we use, and according to the cultural, moral and ideological vantage points from which they are viewed. In a very important sense we construct our experience: how we sense and interpret what happens to us and to the world around us is a function of structures of understanding and perceptual filters that are so culturally embedded that we are scarcely aware of their existence or operation.

The quantity or length of experience is not necessarily connected to its richness or intensity. Because of the habitual ways we draw meaning from our experiences, these experiences can become evidence for the self-fulfilling prophecies that stand in the way of critical insight. Uncritically affirming people's histories, stories and experiences risks idealising and romanticising them. Experiences are neither innocent nor free from the cultural contradictions that inform them.

7.4.4. Learning to Learn

Learning is not just a process of understanding things. But it should be practicalised in real life. The ability of adults to learn how to learn - to become skilled at learning in a range of different situations and through a range of different styles - has often been proposed as an overarching purpose for those educators who work with adults.

Learning involves an epistemological awareness deeper than simply knowing how one scores on a cognitive style inventory, or what is one's typical or preferred pattern of learning. Rather, it means that adults possess a self-conscious awareness of how it is they come to know what they know; an awareness of the reasoning, assumptions, evidence and justifications that underlie our beliefs that something is true.

Learning to learn is a skill that exists far beyond academic boundaries is evident from the research conducted on practical intelligence and everyday cognition in settings and activities as diverse as grocery shopping and betting shops. The connections between a propensity for learning how to learn and the nature of the learning task or domain also need clarification. Learning how to learn is much more frequently spoken of in studies of clearly defined skill development or knowledge acquisition, and much less frequently referred to in studies examining emotional learning or the development of emotional intelligence.

7.5. Emergent Trends

In 1990, three trends in adult learning have emerged, and that promise to exercise some influence into the twenty first century, concern (1) the cross-cultural dimensions of adult learning, (2) adults' engagement in practical theorising, and (3) the ways in which adults learn within the systems of education (distance education, computer assisted instruction, open learning systems) that are linked to recent technological advances.

7.5.1. Cross Cultural Adult Learning

The area of cross-cultural adult learning is still meager. However, the variable of ethnicity is being taken with increasing seriousness. Framing discussions of cultural diversity around a simple binary split between white and non-white populations vastly oversimplifies a complex reality. Among ethnic groups themselves there are significant intra and inter-group tensions.

Adult educators from the dominant American, European and northern cultures will need to examine some of their assumptions, inclinations and preferences about 'natural' adult learning and adult teaching styles. For the among tribes people from the mountains of Laos who are used to working cooperatively and to looking to their teachers for direction and guidance, ways of working that emphasise self-directedness and that place the locus of control with the individual student will be experienced, initially at least, as dissonant and anxiety-producing. However, their liking for materials that focus on personal concrete experience fits well with the adult education practices that emphasise experiential approaches.

Teaching their own' is a common theme surfaced in case studies of multicultural learning. In other words, when adults are taught by educators drawn from their own ethnic communities they tend to feel more comfortable and to do better. Ethnocentric theories and assumptions regarding adult learning styles underscore the need for mainstream adult educators to research their own practice with native and aboriginal peoples. This will require a critically responsive stance towards their practice and a readiness to examine some of their most strongly held, paradigmatic assumptions.

7.5.2. Practical Theorising

Practical theorising has its origins in practitioners' attempts to grapple with the dilemmas, tensions and contradictions of their work. Actions educators take in these situations often appear instinctual. Yet, on reflection, these apparently instinctive reactions can be understood to be embedded in assumptions, readings and interpretations that practitioners have evolved over time to make sense of their practice.

Practitioners seem to come to a more informed understanding of their informal patterns of reasoning by subjecting these to critical review drawing on two important sources. First, they compare their emerging informal theories to those of their colleagues. This happens informally in individual conversations and in a more structured way through participation in reflection groups. Colleagues serve as reflective mirrors in these groups; they reflect back to the practitioner readings of her or his behaviour that come as an interesting surprise. As they describe their own reactions and experiences dealing with typical crises, colleagues can help the individual worker re-frame, broaden and refine her own theories of practice.

Practitioners also use formal theory as a lens through which to view their own actions and the assumptions that inform these. As well as providing multiple perspectives on familiar situations, formal theory can help educators 'name' their practice by illuminating the general elements of what were thought of as idiosyncratic experiences. These two sources - colleagues' experiences and formal theory - intersect continuously in a dialectical interplay of particular and universal perspectives.

7.5.3. Distance Learning

Distance education is regarded as an important setting within which a great deal of significant adult learning occurs. Weekend college formats, multi-media experimentations and the educational possibilities unleashed by satellite broadcasting have combined to provide learning opportunities for millions of adults across the world. That adult educational themes of empowerment, critical reflection, experience and collaboration can inform distance learning activities is evident from case studies of practice that are emerging.

7.6. Conclusion

Adult education is given to those who cannot go for regular education procedures. Education in adolescence is a different approach to empower the illiterate. Through this process, the illiterate poor will get an opportunity to alleviate ignorance. Illiteracy is the main cause of exploitation. When they get education, they will also realise the duplicities in life and protect themselves from adversities causes from ignorance.

References

Brockett R.G, Hiemstra R., *Self-direction in Adult Learning: Perspectives on Theory, Research, and Practice,* Routledge, New York, 1991.

Brookfield S.D., *Understanding and Facilitating Adult Learning,* Jossey-Bass, San Francisco, 1986.

________________., "The development of critical reflection in adulthood", *New Education,* 1991.

Candy P.C., *Self-direction for Lifelong Learning: A Comprehensive Guide to Theory and Practice,* Jossey-Bass, San Francisco, 1990.

Cassara B (ed.), *Adult Education in a Multicultural Society,* Routledge, New York, 1990.

Collins M., "Self-directed learning or an emancipatory practice of adult education: Re-thinking the role of the adult educator", *Proceedings of the 29th Annual Adult Education Research Conference,* Faculty of Continuing Education, University of Calgary, 1988.

Ekpenyong L E., "Studying adult learning through the history of knowledge", *International Journal of Lifelong Education,* 1990.

Hammond M, Collins R., *Self-directed learning: Critical Practice,* Kogan Page, London, 1991.

8

Adult Learning Theories

8.1. Introduction

People start their education at the very younger age and it continues till they acquire the ability to find a job with that education. But unfortunately, all people in a country will not go for education. A lot of factors, including socio-economic, affect education of many and prevented them from regular form of education. For attaining knowledge, go for education in their adolescence. It is known as adult learning.

Adult learning is different from that of child learning. The child education model referred to as pedagogy, places the ultimate responsibility for learning on the teacher. The teacher determines what the student should learn and how and when the material is taught, and has the final say on whether learning has occurred. The pedagogical model is based on the assumption that the teacher is an expert and that students have little to offer to the learning environment.

Adult learners bring a wealth of experience to the training environment. Besides, they have a complex set of needs and presentation requirements that must be fulfilled for learning to occur. One of the most respected names in andragogy-the theory and practice of adult learning-is Malcolm Knowles.

The four principles put forward by Knowles are at the heart of Knowledge Impact's design model. All of our training deliverables have been designed to ensure compliance with these four basic tenets. The following outline describes how Knowledge Impact designed our deliverables to comply with these adult learning principles.

1. Adults need to be involved in the planning and evaluation of their instruction.
   - Interview "power users" identified by the client to gain background information and determine the scope of the training.
   - Provide multiple navigation controls that empower students to pursue their own learning path.
   - Include review questions and exercises throughout the training that provide students with immediate feedback on their learning progress.
   - Include mastery tests for clients that are concerned about certification.
2. Experiences (including mistakes) provide the basis for learning activities.
   - Include simulations that give students the opportunity to perform tasks in a safe practice environment and then apply their new knowledge immediately.
   - Provide multiple levels of feedback that guide students to the correct actions.
3. Adults are most interested in learning subjects that have immediate relevance to their job or personal life.
   - Customise all deliverables to reflect the client's business processes.
   - Work closely with clients to build workflows, examples and scenarios that represent the day-to-day lives of their end-users.
   - Include best practices that detail the client's preferred business processes.
4. Adult learning is problem-centered rather than content-oriented.
   - Include simulations that present the student with role-based scenarios built around the real tasks they'll need to perform on the job.
   - Place tasks in a real-world context to create learning that the student can use immediately.

In the process of learning, adults follow certain basic concepts. But, the typical adult learning theories encompass the basic concepts of behavioural change and experience. From there, complexities begin to diverge specific theories and concepts in an eclectic borage of inferences. Up until 1950's, the basic definitions of learning were built around the idea of change in behaviour. After this point more complexities were introduced "such as whether one needs to perform in order for learning to have occurred or whether all human behavior is learned."

Relating to age, there are "four invariant stages of cognitive development. Normal children will reach the final stage of development, which is the stage of formal operations, between the age of twelve and fifteen.

In adult learning theory, humanism, personal responsibility orientation, behaviourism, neobehaviorism, critical perspectives, and constructivism are all important facets and perspectives. The most common treatments of the research of these areas of self-directed adult learning are learning projects, qualitative studies, and quantitative measures. Collins explores adult learning as the interactive relationship of theory and practice. In basic terms, the adult learner studies a particular theory and then puts it into practice when presented with the opportunity to do so. Thus, the understanding of an adult learning theory can prompt practice and practice can prompt adult learning theory revision.

The theory of adult learning is divided into two elements:

a) A process that creates change within the individual, and
b) A process to infuse change into the organisation.

There are significant, identifiable differences between adult learners and learners under the age of eighteen. Primarily, the differences, according to Knowles, relate to an adult learner being more self-directing, having a repertoire of experience, and being internally motivated to learn subject matter that can be applied immediately - learning that is especially "closely related to the developmental tasks of his or her social role."

8.2. Andragogy

To educate adults is not an easy task. It needs patience and perseverance. The term Andragogy means "the art and science of helping adults learn." Knowles labelled andragogy as an emerging technology which facilitates the development and implementation of learning activities for adults.

The three keys to transformational learning, according to Merriam and Caffarella, are experience, critical reflection and development. The aspect of experience seems like an important consideration in creating an effective learning opportunity for adults. The learning opportunity needs to be relevant and applicable to a person's set of experiences.

Adults should think critically. This critical reflection is the other key to transformational learning and part of andragogy's self-directed learning. Reflection/think time is yet another essential principle to creating an effective learning experience for adults. Adult learners need time to contemplate the ramifications of the learning experience to their experience and responsibilities.

Development is another key to transformational learning. The ability to think critically, which is mandatory to effecting a transformation, is itself developmental. If development is the outcome of transformational learning, then an effective adult learning opportunity needs to be created that will take personal development into consideration.

Improvement in individual skill and knowledge as well as developing organisational performance by transfer of learning directly to work applications is the objectives of adult learning. To attain this, the learners should follow problem-based learning which seeks to increase problem-solving and critical thinking skills; cooperative learning, which builds communication and interpersonal skills; and situated learning, which targets specific technical skills that can be directly related to the field of work. Each of these methods support the assumptions about how adults learn; specifically they are more self-directed, have a need for direct application to their work, and are able to contribute more to collaborative learning through their experience.

8.3. Multiple Intelligences

There are a lot of theories prevailing in the field of adult education. However, Howard Gardner represents those theorists who have dismissed the idea of one type of intelligence as typically measured by today's psychometric instruments. He posited that there were seven (later eight) types of intelligences:

- — Linguistic intelligence
- — Logical-mathematical intelligence
- — Spatial intelligence or the ability to form a mental model of the spatial world and to maneuver within it using this model
- — Musical intelligence
- — Bodily-kinesthetic intelligence, or the ability to solve problems using one's body as performed by athletes, dancers and other craftspeople
- — Interpersonal intelligence or the ability to understand other people
- — Intrapersonal intelligence or the ability to understand one's self

The first two are the types of intelligence commonly measured by IQ tests, and which are commonly accepted as "intelligence." Gardner later added an eighth intelligence to his taxonomy, Naturalist Intelligence, which he defined as "expertise in the recognition and classification of the numerous species - the flora and fauna—of his or her environment" Sternberg's Triarchic Theory can be viewed as an interpretation of intelligence as information processing.

8.4. Conditions/Environment

For some people, circumstances may become the main villain on the path of their educational life. In other words, situational circumstances constitute an environment that promotes or discourages learning. Those circumstances may be created by organisational structure, positive or negative environmental situations, or time constraints. The learning capabilities of organisational members are, at least in part, socially constructed by national, occupational, or other institutions. Internal boundaries are established by specialities or departments within the framework of organisations that hinder cross-boundary learning.

Positive outcomes are much more apt to result in a positive and successful learning experience. Pleasant outcomes (successes) reinforce stimulus-response links whereas unpleasant outcomes (failures) break stimulus-response links. As a result, pleasant outcomes are much more effective at teaching new behaviours. This concept follows the transformational leadership theory providing positive opportunities for individuals to grow within the framework of organisational life.

In adult learning, we can choose practical training. But the learning processes that require practice are much slower than those that do not require practice. Time consideration is an important element in considering the process of learning within an organisation that must meet specific deadlines or has a client base that needs to be managed continuously. The conditions may not be suitable for an elaborate training or educational programme. Organisations must consider time pressure as a tool that can encourage learning and speed up processes.

8.5. Experiential Learning

Experience is the true teacher in everybody's life. Experiential Learning Theory also emphasises the role that true experiences play in the learning process. It is this emphasis that distinguishes itself from other learning theories. Cognitive learning theories emphasise cognition over affect and behavioral learning theories deny any role for subjective experience in the learning process.

Experiential learning is a sort of learning which enables students to apply newly acquired knowledge in a relevant setting. The relevant setting can be a sponsored institution of learning with trainers, instructors, teachers, or professors to guide the lesson. Experiential learning can be also defined as education that occurs as a direct participation in the events of life. Thus, learning is not achieved in a formal setting, but in the practice of reflection of daily experiences.

Kolb furthers the second definition of experiential learning by developing a model which details learning process through experiences. Kolb and Fry's experiential learning model is a continuous spiral process which consists of four basic elements:

a) Concrete experience

b) Observation and reflection

c) Forming abstract concepts

d) Testing in new situations

Immediate or concrete experiences are the basis for observation and reflections. These reflections are assimilated and distilled into abstract concepts from which new implications for action can be drawn. According to Kolb and Fry, the adult learner can enter the process at any one of the elements.

8.6. Anxiety and the Adult Learner

The minds of adults pester with many anxieties. Organisations must find a method to deal with the anxiety adults experience when they are forced to "unlearn" what they know and learn something new. The common annoying anxieties among adults are learning anxiety and survival anxiety. Learning will only happen when survival anxiety is greater than learning anxiety. Each of these anxieties could be managed, for example learning can be constructed in a "safe" environment where the consequences of failure are minimal. Survival anxiety can obviously be increased by threatening job loss, a lack of security, or recognising competitive elements of the market.

8.7. Jarvis's Learning Process and Adult Learning Theory

Adults have a lot of experiences in their life. Truly, these experiences are the biggest knowledge one can attain in their life. More over, this is one of the most significant qualities unique to adult learning as compared to that of children, teens, and traditional college students. That experience offers adult learners a meaningful advantage in the learning process. The sum of those experiences provides many reference points for exploration, new application, and new learning.

Experience is the beginning of all learning. Real learning begins when a response is called for in relation to an experience. If an individual is unchanged by a situation, Jarvis questions whether real learning has taken place. He proposes that new experiences need to be experimented with, evaluated, reflected upon and reasoned about for the most effective change and therefore learning to take place. These post experience behaviours culminate in the best and highest form of learning where change and increased experience have happened. Jarvis's model offers an excellent learning model that can assist both facilitators and learners in advancing education and learning situations.

The universe is the biggest university and we learn something from each and every people whom we meet in daily life. Learning from an older or more experienced mentor provides an incredibly valuable learning forum and support network. Listening, and learning from a mentor's successes, failures, or mistakes can help expand one's knowledge base and shorten learning cycles experience alone would require. Living largely out of one's personal experiences also short-circuits meaningful, relational connections that expand one's horizons and better equip one to succeed in this world and avoid so many of its pitfalls.

8.8. Conclusion

Adult learners come to learning with a wide range of previous experiences, knowledge, self-direction, interests, and competencies. This diversity must be accommodated in the professional development planning. In order to effectively design courses meant for adult students, it is necessary to understand how adults learn, and especially how their needs differ from those of children. Most of the adult learning theories are based on the work of Malcolm Knowles, who introduced the term andragogy to describe the art and science of helping adults to learn. Certainly the field of adult learning theory demands scholarly research.

References

Knox, Alan, *Adult Development and Learning*, San Francisco: Jossey-Bass, 1977.

Lones, Paul S., "Learning as Creativity: Implications for Adult Learners", *Adult Learning*, 2000.

Merriam, S.B., *An Update on Adult Learning Theory*, New York: Greenwood Press, 1993.

————————., and R. Caffarella, *Learning in Adulthood: A Comprehensive Guide*, San Francisco: Jossey Bass, 1999.

9

Methods and Techniques in Adult Education

9.1. Introduction

Adult education is the outcome of thoughtful and theoretical framework. Methods and techniques have an important place in the adult learning process and it summarise the range of practical strategies used today in the field of adult education, and attempted to determine the contribution of educational techniques in the learning experience of the adult learner by identifying the critical factors that would make such experience a valuable, lasting and effective one.

Education has certainly some objectives. The selection, application and mastering of a particular technique only address the "How" of the educational goal, and cannot be analysed outside of an overall framework that includes the role that the "Why", "What", "Where" and "Who" plays in the overall educational process. The "Why" relates to the objective and justifies the educational experience as a desire to be educated. The "What" relates to content and the type of knowledge being expanded in the educational process, i.e. emotional, cognitive and/or spiritual. The "Where" investigates the places where the meeting of educators, students and subject-matter take place. The "Who" acknowledges the duality of educator and learner as drivers of the educational process and the influence of these agents in the selection of the most appropriate techniques. From an educator's perspective, learning reaches its plateau when the delivery technique is perfectly aligned with the requirements of the remaining "W's".

9.2. Dynamic Equilibrium of Learning

Learning is not an easy matter. It is interrelated between certain variables. The dynamic interdependence among four key elements involved in the educational process which function as a system:

i) Learner
ii) Educator
iii) Subject-matter
iv) Technique

The learning ability of a learner is correlated with the educator, the subject for studying and the techniques used. However, they operate at the same level. Firstly, educator and learner work as elements that take action in the learning experience, and secondly, content and delivery methods work as the subject-matter(s) and tools required to make the experience effective.

9.2.1. Learner

The combined interaction between educator and learner through content and execution method is dynamic and non-repeatable. In order to remain at this "learning plateau" throughout the learning experience, it has to be recognised that all four elements have to change during this evolution. It is impossible for any of them to remain constant and keep the educational experience optimal.

9.2.2. Educator

The educators should be store of information. Self-knowledge determines the very basic building blocks for commitment, love and mastery of teaching. It is not only required that the teacher be proficient in the subjects and techniques about to be shared, but also that a strong inner-sense of self-identity and integrity be present. The learning experience will reflect the very soul of that individual. The inner landscape of teaching itself is then the place to explore and to find an answer to the techniques required for each point in time and space, to manage/teach/learn content effectively.

9.2.3. Subject Matter

The teachers should very talented. Any subject matter should be viewed from the intellectual, emotional and spiritual dimensions not as segmented aspects but in the wholeness of reality. Bad teachers distance themselves from the subject they are teaching- and in the process, from their students. Good teachers join self and subject and students in the fabric of life. Good teachers possess a capacity for connectedness. They are able to weave a complex weave of connections, among themselves, their subjects and their students so that students can learn to weave a world for themselves.

9.2.4. Techniques

Techniques have a defined life-cycle. When conditions change, they should expire and be replaced by new ones as learners, educators and content evolve. The challenge becomes for the educator, some times with the help of the learning community of students, to continuously be able to select the most appropriate techniques throughout the process objectively given that she/he is part of the system itself.

9.3. Prerequisites of the Teacher

A good teacher leads a person into light and the bad ones lead them into darkness. The teacher acts as the element of the learning process who exercises the intentional act of creating conditions that can help students learn. She/he should learn to "re-educate her/his heart" so it gets engaged in the joyful "pursuit of truth in the company of friends." Among other simple issues that may characterise a teacher here are some collected from our own experience as teachers:

i) A clear sense of identity with our culture, our country, family, our own genes, strengths and weaknesses. Identity comes from the self-knowledge of our examined life.

ii) A humble integrity that help us to face reality with honesty and courage; that allows us to be vulnerable, take risks and to expose our weaknesses. Integrity comes as an inner decision that upraises the elemental need for our own beliefs to guide our life.

iii) An educated heart able to remain open in the very moments when it is asked to hold more, to understand, to be patient, to be silent or to talk.

iv) A spiritual quest for connectedness with our subject of study, our selves, our students and the world.

v) An authentic respect for the students as complex and sacred beings capable of enriching our connections with the subject of study, the learning community and the world.

vi) A welcome to the voices of truth, in the way of listening to the voices of the students, and their silences as well; to the stories narrated as experiences that connect the subject-matter with reality; also listening to our own speaking voice when we teach, and to the inner voice that guide us on what technique to use.

vii) An aptitude for asking good questions and listening. Learning not to ask the questions too soon, and giving a silent space, even if the heart fears the silence.

viii) A willingness to take the risk of inviting open dialogue without knowing where it is going to take us, and the knowledge of how to turn the questions into a communal dialogue, trusting that the community can deal with the issue at hand, because "truth is an eternal conversation about things that matter, conducted with passion and discipline."

9.4. Understanding Adult Learners

The students of adult learning are adults and they possess certain specific mind sets. They are not the regular students like in formal education. Adult students share some important characteristics. They are active learners who respond positively to learning experiences that involve them. They like to have their opinions consulted and "enjoy having their talents and experience made use of in the teaching situation."

For the purposes of understanding the influence of the adult learners in the selection of techniques, two aspects of adults are briefly discussed:

a) The characteristics of the adult learner

b) The learning styles

9.4.1. Characteristics of the Adult Learner

In 1968, Knowles popularised the term andragogy. Here, he

reflected on four key areas where adults display certain characteristics that govern the learning process, and makes this process different than children's education. Even though Knowles' conceptualisation has been criticised by other education theorists they would still help us to address our question on the appropriate methodologies to the adult learner. For Knowles, the four areas that govern adult learning are the following:

i) Changes in self-concept
ii) The role of experience
iii) Readiness to learn
iv) Orientation to learning

9.4.2. Learning Styles

Unlike children, the Adults act as according to their own direction. They have a vast knowledge from their pool of experience also. Their willingness to learn and orientation are also high comparing to that of children. But beyond the four specific characteristics of adult learners, several experts in the field maintain that we as learners have a certain tendency to manage knowledge and reflect, act, theorise about it in different ways. For instance, Kolb identifies four learning styles. As learners display more propensities to learn according to a certain style, it is possible to recognise four learner types:

i) *Accommodator*: ability to learn for hands-on experience. Learn by doing.
ii) *Diverger*: best at viewing concrete situations from many different points of view.
iii) *Converger*: individuals within learning style proficient at finding practical uses for ideas and theories.
iv) *Assimilator*: best at understanding a wide range of information and putting into concise logical form.

9.4.2.1. Determining Content

The selection of content is very important in adult education. Political, social and economic movements within reigning and new paradigms have historically defined content at macro-social levels. The three major tendencies, which evolved as key influences for determining content in the formal and non-formal adult education are:

i) *Professional development and training*: emphasis on corporate development, automation and training techniques for the professional achievements in the global age.

ii) *Social focus*: emphasis on social justice, democracy, citizenship, ecology, equal opportunities and non-discrimination issues.

iii) *Self-actualisation and spiritual development*: emphasis on spiritual development and holistic views of daily life, work and education.

9.5. Methodologies and Techniques

The success of adult education also depends on the techniques and methods used for teaching an adult learner. There are specific methods used in teaching, as opposed to other formal agencies of schooling that have employed, and often do employ, methods other than teaching, for example indoctrination, suggestion, threats and force. The teacher does not want to foster merely belief, but to bring it about through the exercise of free rational judgment by the student. Moreover, it is important to recall the key psychological principles advanced by liberal education throughout the 20th century: "progressing from the simple to the complex, from the particular to the general, from the concrete to the abstract."

The analysis of techniques used in adult education generally divides the strategies in three broad categories:

i) Teacher oriented techniques
ii) Interactive techniques
iii) Independent techniques

9.5.1. Teacher Oriented Techniques

Here, the sole responsibility is on the teacher. In the teacher oriented techniques the lecture and the questioning techniques are the most utilised.

9.5.1.1. Lecture

When the subject-matter of study requires specific information, the learning community is large and the place of learning allows it, the lecture is useful. It should be planned in terms of length and placement and should have a structured outline, including an introduction, a body and a conclusion. Ideal lectures give mini-summaries periodically, allow participation of the community, time for reflection and feedback.

9.5.1.2. Interrogative Method

To attain education is an urge for knowing more. It generates questions and will ultimately lead to knowledge. These techniques are a powerful way of increasing student participation. The teacher plans them according to a higher or lower level of response. They could ask for summarising, understanding, encouraging critical thinking, enhancing problem-solving ability or stimulating creativity or research activities.

Students must cultivate questioning mentality. Questions may be open with a wide realm of answers or closed with limited responses. The skilled teacher plans the questions according to the goals and the content, and clearly phrases them to be sure that they don't reveal the answers. After the students answer, the next step requires expertise to know where to place the students' responses. They may help to reinforce the subject-matter, prove it, refocus it, redirect it or rephrase it.

In the classroom, there must be an environment to ask questions, to answer questions and not to feel threatened by giving an incorrect response. The teacher should listen to the students' questions and be sure that she/he and the class understood the question. There are some paths that the teacher can take: answering the question, redirecting the question to the class, helping the student to answer his/her own question, asking the student to stop after class to discuss the question, referring the student to a resource where the question can be answered or deferring the question until a more appropriate time.

9.5.2. Interactive Techniques

Students can use a number of interrogative techniques. The most common techniques are: role-play, case study, group-work, programmed fieldwork and cooperative learning.

9.5.2.1. Discussion Groups

In discussions, all matters, whether positive or negative, are coming. Discussion can target almost any level of cognitive and affective domains but requires a structured process of large and small group discussion focused in the subject-matter objectives.

There are some variations like "circle responses" that gives the opportunity to talk to every one in the small group; "spend a penny" which works with the use of tokens to allow everybody to talk a certain number of times; "brainstorming" that is open to the imagination of the group; "guided discussions" where the group facilitation expertise of the teacher draws out the more reluctant speakers and gently holds back the more verbal participants; "panel discussions" a conversation of a small group in front of the whole group; "debates" a discussion wherein two opposing sides will be moderated; "reaction groups" which constitute a forum for quick responses; and "concentric circles" where a small circle of group members form to discuss a topic within a larger circle that listens for a while until the discussion is reversed.

9.5.2.2. Case Study

It is popular in medicine and legal professions, and it refers to real life problems narrated with a story telling quality and challenges participants to find recommendations and solutions to the problems. They are mainly used in teaching knowledge, values and attitudes.

9.5.2.3. Group Work

Here, students' collective mentality is tested. Group work is a generic term for multiple techniques in which two or more students are assigned a task that involves collaboration and self initiated conversation. Group work is considered vital to education because among other reasons, it offers an embracing affective climate, promotes learner responsibility and autonomy, and is a step toward self directed learning.

9.5.2.4. Programmed Field Work

Observation is another important factor. More than a technique the fieldwork is a learning process that occurs in a natural setting with or without teacher observation. The most important benefit is the opportunity to apply and integrate theory with practice, even if the evaluation process is difficult because of the absence of the teacher, for example in a hospital placement for nursing students.

9.5.2.5. Cooperative Learning

It is a process that involves a group of techniques to work in small peer learning groups to enhance classroom interaction and achieve learning purposes. In order for the students to work cooperatively teachers must systematically structure the basic components, and be available as a resource person to monitor and facilitate group process.

9.5.2.6. Role-playing

The recreation of real life situation is handling here. It involves acting it out in front of the group. It can be spontaneous or guided by the teacher, is useful for the development of interpersonal skills and the affective domain and can induce a real experience of emotions.

9.5.2.7. Simulations and Games

Involving in games stimulate energy and thinking capacity. Simulations and games provide a fun break from the seriousness of our daily life, and allow students to relax and learn painlessly. They represent or model a real life situation in a concrete or abstract form and encourage the use of rules, principles, concepts and decision-making inner processes. Skillful debriefing is necessary to transfer insights into real-life applications.

9.5.3. Independent Techniques

Some independent techniques are also prevailing in the field of education. Among the independent techniques we find computer assisted techniques, programmed and modularised instruction, independent learning packages, and self directed learning techniques.

9.5.3.1. Programmed and Modularised Instruction

These techniques are highly structured printed or computerised programmes in which the content is broken into small sequenced steps. The learner moves through the programme based on supplying answers to questions posed at intervals during the programme. The students work at their own pace and receive immediate feedback to their questions.

9.5.3.2. Independent Learning Packages

The needs of students differ and different students need different learning packages. The independent learning packages consist of independent or prescribed materials selected in consultation with the teacher, according to the student's needs and level. The curriculum can be tailor made for each individual.

9.5.3.3. Self- Directed Learning Techniques

It is a process by which the learner develops a plan for learning that includes goals, resources, strategies and evaluations. This plan is made in consultation with the teacher who acts as facilitator of the process. The student enters into a learning contract with the teacher to ensure that the requirements for a particular course of study are met.

9.6. Conclusion

Universe is the vast educational institute and the entire lifespan of a person is his educational period. However, the right time of acquiring knowledge is the childhood and early stages of young age. Adult education is therefore a difficult task because the mentality of the students will be totally different. But, with simple learning process and effortless techniques, teachers can enter into the hearts of these illiterate adult folks.

References

Kolb, D., *Learning Style Inventory*, McBer & Co., 1976.

Mezei, K., *Principles of Adult Learning*, Humber College Ed., Toronto, 1991.

Renner P., "The Art of Teaching Adults: How to become an exceptional instructor and facilitator", Training Associates, Vancouver, BC, Canada, 1999.

10

Adult Education in India

India has always given priority to education. While the British rule, India once again realised the importance of education. During those times, India suffered a lot and the top positions were handled by the British people. When India got independence, the government gave first priority to uplift the educational standard of the people. The Constitution of India directs the state to make provision for securing the right of children to education within the limits of its economic capacity, and to provide free and compulsory education to all children upto the age of 14 by 1960. It also lay down that the state shall promote with special care the educational and economic interests of the weaker sections of the people such as Scheduled Castes and Scheduled Tribes.

The problem of illiteracy was the biggest menace India witnessed after independence. The number of people who got higher education was very marginal. To betterment the educational status of the people, India undertook a series of programmes. Adult education was one among these programmes. This was followed by the centre based programme under the National Adult Education Programme from 1978 to 1990 by which time the National Literacy Mission had come into existence and based on the initial success of the campaign approach, the same was accepted as the dominant strategy for adult education programmes in India.

10.1. Education Programmes in India

10.1.1. Gram Shikshan Mohim Movement

The government's effort to educate the illiterate received massive support from the nooks and corners from India. By taking the responsibility, state governments also organised a number of programmes. In 1959, the state of Maharashtra started Gram Shikshan Mohim movement. It was a step towards mass mobilisation in the field of adult education and was launched on an experimental basis in 25 districts of the state. The programme was of a very short duration and there was no systematic follow-up as a result of which there was large scale relapse of neo-literates into illiterates.

10.1.2. Farmers' Functional Literacy Projects

In India, people who opt agriculture as their livelihood kept off from education. To provide education to this section, India organised Farmers' Functional Literacy Project as part of the Green Revolution with the objective of making farmers functionally literate in high yielding cultivation areas. The three components of this programme were: functional literacy, farmers' training and radio programmes for the farmers. Although the long term objective was to establish one project in each district, by 1977 only 140 projects could be covered. This programme had to be discontinued due to very small coverage and lack of financial support.

10.1.3. Workers' Education

India is a poor country and poverty instigates many people to go for work in a very younger age. To educate the working class, India implemented this programme. It is implemented through the Central Board of Workers' Education and its institutes. However, the efforts under this scheme could not be linked to the literacy schemes/projects being funded under the departments of Education of the states or by the Govt. of India. The scheme of Shramik Vidyapeeths of the Department of Education, Govt. of India is a small scheme in urban areas which links literacy with vocational programmes but on a very limited scale of intervention.

10.1.4. Non-formal Education for Youth

Youth is the backbone of every nation. They determine the economic welfare of a country. To uplift the conditions of youths, Indian government implemented non-formal education for youths in 1975. The objective of this programme was to provide young people relevant to their environment. It aimed at increasing functional skills of the learners so as to increase their productivity and social participation. On an experimental basis, one project each was started in 100 districts but it received a setback due to inadequate financial allocations.

10.2. Education Commission

Illiteracy is a curse. The future of a nation depends on the intellectually aware and highly educated people. Reiterating the importance of education, India appointed an Education Commission (1964-66), which was a significant event in the history of education in India. Among several measures, it recommended that high priority be accorded to the liquidation of illiteracy. It urged that adult education should be promoted both through "selective" as well as "mass approach" and stressed on the active involvement of teachers and students and the wider use of media for the literacy programme.

In the world of science and technology, the main objective of education should be to relate it to the life, needs and aspirations of the people so as to make it an instrument of socioeconomic and political change. The first nationwide attempt at eradication of illiteracy was made through the National Adult Education Programme (1978), to follow up the recommendations of the Education Commission Report and the subsequent National Policy on Education (1968) announced by the Government of India.

10.2.1. National Adult Education Programme (NAEP)

India considered that the upper class people have the priority to go for education. Those who enjoy the higher positions in religion discouraged the lower castes from education very strongly. So a large number of people were kept out of education. A massive programme of Adult Education called the National Adult Education Programme (NAEP) for removal of illiteracy in the 15-35 age group was formulated by the Government of India and launched on 2nd October, 1978. The target for this programme was to educate 100 million adults within a time frame of five years.

Imparting literacy was not the only objective of the National Adult Education Programme. But it also aims to give the learners with functionality and awareness which were conceived as three integral components of this programme. Literacy meant acquisition of the skills of reading, writing and numeracy. Functionality implied the ability to utilise and apply the skills so acquired in day to day life with a view to promote efficiency of the neo-literate. The social awareness component aimed at knowing, understanding and taking action on issues which affect the individual, the community and the society, so as to improve their quality of life.

10.2.2. Rural Functional Literacy Project (RFLP)

People living in hinterlands were very unlucky while considering education. The educational institutions were not in the reach of those people. To educate the people in the rural areas, India undertook Rural Functional Literacy Project in 1978. The erstwhile 144 Farmers' Functional Literacy Projects and 60 Nonformal Education Projects were merged into it. Further projects were added and the number of projects throughout the country in 1987 were 513, each having upto a maximum number of 300 adult education centres, each centre having 25-30 learners.

10.2.3. State Adult Education Programme (SAEP)

Besides central government, the states also implemented a lot of programmes to educate the adults. The states took up centre based projects under the state plan funds on the lines of RFLPs.

10.2.4. Through Voluntary Agencies

With an aim to spread education among the people, some voluntary organisations are also implementing certain programmes. To ensure greater participation of voluntary agencies, the Central Scheme of Assistance to Voluntary Agencies was revived in April 1982. Under this scheme, registered societies were sanctioned Centre-based projects for functional literacy and post literacy and they were allowed to run the projects in a compact area.

10.2.5. National Literacy Mission (NLM)

The storm of educational revival was not restricted within a certain place. Instead, it was a feeling aroused in the minds of every people in India. The National Literacy Mission was set up by the Government of India in recognition of the need for priority attention to literacy for speeding up the development process and was launched by the Prime Minister of India on 5th May, 1988. The objective of the National Literacy Mission in quantitative terms was, to start with, to impart functional literacy to 80 million adult illiterate persons in the age group 15-35. This target has since been revised to making 100 million persons literate during the VIII Five Year Plan i.e. between 1992 and 1997. The NLM has adopted a campaign approach, the success of which rests on the mobilisation of social forces and on securing people's participation.

10.2.6. Centre-based Approach

Improving the educational status of people, India divided the responsibility to the state and district governance. At the same time, the government also undertook some central based programmes also. The National Literacy Mission which was set up in 1988 took over the National Adult Education Programme as it was conceptualised in 1978. The National Adult Education Programme followed the centre- based approach under the Rural Functional Literacy Projects. The centre-based approach consisted of one Rural Functional Literacy Project of 300, 200 or 100 centres and almost each district had one project sanctioned to it. Each centre run by one paid instructor was to cater to 30 learners. However, for hilly and remote areas the number of learners per centre could be less.

National Literacy Mission is a continuing process. The post literacy and continuing education has been an evolving strategy. It has been recognised at the national level that there can be no format or strategy which would be uniformly applicable all over. The strategies adopted by different states may vary. This is so because each project has to take into account the specificity of the district, achievement levels of learners in the literacy phase, learners' needs and aspirations keeping in view their social and living conditions as well as the objectives which can be reasonably set for the project keeping in mind the material and human resources which are available and can be mobilised for the project. Based on the experience gained so far in implementing post literacy projects in different parts of the country, an outline of a strategy for implementation of post literacy campaigns has been endorsed by the NLM.

With political will, the society took the responsibility of the National Literacy Mission for the achievement of the Mission's goals which were to be achieved in a time bound manner. It was set up with the objective of making 80 million persons functionally literate by the year 1995. The launching of the Mission therefore led to a review of all the ongoing programmes at that time.

Rural parts of India were the worst affected places while conducting educations. Rural areas lack institutions for educating the people. So, the scheme of Rural Functional Literacy Projects was reorganised in March, 1988 on the eve of setting up of the National Literacy Mission. The changes which were brought about in the reorganisation mainly consisted of streamlining the various activities and correcting managerial deficiencies.

Administrative and supervisory control was vested with the State Governments and UTs and they were required to lay down norms and procedures for selection, training and placement of different categories of project functionaries. The reorganised projects also envisaged Project Advisory Committees which were supposed to advise the project officials regarding the location and organisation of adult education centres, bringing the needs of the local community to the notice of the project officials, ensuring coordination with development departments, reviewing and monitoring the implementation of the project etc.

The National Education Programme was also not free from deficiencies. The report of the Public Accounts Committee for the period 1985-90 pointed out a large number of deficiencies in the implementation of the Rural Functional Literacy Projects particularly relating to the appointment of permanent project staff in violation of the guidelines, incurring of avoidable extra expenditure, inadequate training, non-supply/delayed supply of teaching learning materials, lack of adequate monitoring of implementation of the projects from the 0level of the Ministry, lack of adequate involvement of the State Governments and UTs, absence of Project Advisory Committees as envisaged in the project guidelines etc.

The single most important aspect of the inadequacy of the Rural Functional Literacy Projects was the fact that conceptually the Rural Functional Literacy Projects were minuscule programmes in very small project areas and coverage of the entire district or a selected area was not even thought of. There was no concept of involvement of the community or creating an environment for literacy and generation of demand. The mode of implementation was through a bureaucratic process and structure. The teaching learning period was excessively long leading to substantial dropouts.

The mushrooming growth of voluntary agencies from 1978 onwards was another aspect. At one point of time, nearly 650 voluntary agencies were receiving assistance for implementing the centre based programmes under the honorarium payment mode. Encouragement to such agencies, many of which later turned out to be agencies on paper, led to large scale misuse of funds and malpractice and defaming of the centre based programme as well as the National Adult Education Programme. Although many adverse evaluation reports and audit objections were received, not enough attention was paid to the ability of voluntary agencies to implement such programmes and selection of really good voluntary agencies.

10.2.7. Campaign Approach

Campaign is the best method to materialise any ideas to the people. It has a wider acceptability. One notable exception to the centre-based approach and an experiment with the campaign mode was first seen in Kottayam city in Kerala where the District Collector, by mobilising 200 volunteers from Mahatma Gandhi University, and forging links with the 2000 non-literates in 6-60 age-group in the city, succeeded in making them fully literate within three months. But, the real breakthrough came, not out of wisdom internal to the NLM but with an experiment in mass literacy campaign initiated in 1989 and successfully completed in 1990 in Ernakulum district in Kerala. This was not a government sponsored programme implemented by the District Administration but under the leadership provided by the District

Literacy Society which had a few persons from the District Administration but also people from all different sections and back-grounds.

Kerala put forward the campaign for total literacy in Ernakulam district. This campaign witnessed a fusion between the district administration headed by its Collector, voluntary groups, social activists and others, and was spearheaded by the Kerala Shastra Sahitya Parishad (KSSP). Ernakulam achieved this objective on 4th February, 1990 and along with it the unique distinction of being the first district in the country to become 'fully' literate. Ernakulam declared itself 'totally literate' and that declaration led to the launching of a statewide campaign in Kerala, a campaign more challenging in size and complexity. The Kerala State Literacy Campaign covered 18 lakh persons in the age group of 6-60 years within a span of one year.

Later, the Ernakulam model Total Literacy Programme campaign extended to Malappuram district of Kerala. But, the Mallapuram Pilot Project failed largely due to lack of sufficient ground work. The other experiment was the 19th Century experiment in the then princely States of Travancore and Cochin. In these princely States the programme was taken up after creation of demand for literacy.

The Ernakulam experiment proved to be a breakthrough and established the feasibility of a mass-based, community-based, campaign approach with the objective of generating environment building and demand for literacy followed by literacy instruction. Subsequently sanctioned campaigns have all attempted to replicate, by and large, the strategy and the various phases and processes in the Ernakulam campaign.

With the success of total literacy campaign in Ernakulam, the programme was extended to 13 districts of Kerala, Dakshin Kannada and Bijapur in Karnataka, Chittoor and Nellore in Andhra Pradesh, Midnapur and Burdwan in West Bengal and the Union Territory of Pondicherry. The launching of these TLCs had a snow-balling effect. A perusal of literacy campaign proposals from the districts of Kerala, Pondicherry UT and others which were placed before the Executive Committee of NLM, shows that the proposals merely mention that they are submitted for campaigns based on the model of the Ernakulam experiment.

The Ernakulam campaign strategy was adopted as such by the NLMA in other districts and projects which were taken up and funds were released for implementation. As of August 1994, the Executive Committee of the NLM had approved literacy campaigns in as many as 275 districts and post-literacy campaigns in as many as 100 districts. The basic model in all these literacy campaign projects is the same as in the Ernakulam campaign.

Campaigns for total literacy are the mode of programme implementation. Today, a set of guidelines were also formulated by the NLM. These guidelines, however, are not viewed as prescriptive or sacrosanct but as suggested principles to enable planners to think through the objectives and the processes involved in the formulation and implementation of the project plans.

10.2.8. Nationwide Propaganda

Propaganda is another method of spreading literacy mission. Initially, NLM placed emphasis on non-governmental organisations and creation of a general ambience or environment for literacy by Kala Jathas or cultural caravans in different parts of the country. The entire process was set in motion through a non-governmental organisation called the Bharat Gyan Vigyan Samiti in August, 1989, followed by a countrywide cultural literacy campaign in the International Literacy Year during October 1990 known as Bharat Gyan Vigyan Jathas (BGVJs). While these Jathas had to contend with major caste and communal events, nevertheless it placed literacy as an issue before the people and on the national agenda.

The involvement of thousands of politicians, administrators, educators, media persons taken together with the demand for literacy programmes generated in the villages brought literacy on to the political agenda of the nation as well. The BGVS brought together a number of voluntary organisations and service associations, youth, students groups, women's movement and adult educators. Their network through the Jathas made literacy work a personal and common organisational priority for millions all over the country.

During the early years of the National Literacy Mission, the organisational structure of the literacy campaign in the districts, beginning from Kerala was inclined towards the BGVS. It played a major role in the districts of Kerala and in some other districts which were having high literacy rates and were taken up initially. Whereas the real problem of illiteracy is seen in the low literacy rate districts of the northern belt in the country especially in the States of Bihar, M.P., Rajasthan and U.P., which together with A.P., Maharashtra and West Bengal constitute the majority of illiterates in India.

To build confidence it is necessary that such high literacy districts be taken up first, since it is easy to show results in such areas, it is much more important to face the major challenge where it lies rather than take credit for covering a large number of districts in the high literacy areas. Yet, this is precisely what happened between 1990 and 1993 in which period only 33 projects out of a total of 138 projects were sanctioned to the four major Hindi-speaking States. In fact, one gets the impression that systematic planning was not done to cover the districts in the four major Hindi-speaking States but the campaigns were pushed in the high literacy and easier districts elsewhere in the country.

10.3. Recent Initiatives

10.3.1. Emphasis on Low Literate States

The districts having low literacy rate also followed the trend happened in high literate states. It was only from May 1993 that the trend really shifted from high literacy rate districts to the low literacy rate districts of the northern belt of Hindi speaking States. In these districts, voluntary work is difficult and so District Collectors and their machinery have had to be involved for mobilisation and motivation efforts. Even in such districts, the TLCs are being launched by voluntary organisations called Zilla Saksharata Samitis which generally consist of social activists, Government officials, representatives of Panchayat Samitis, District Boards, women activists, educationists, Principals, teachers and other leading members of the community.

The thrust of the National Literacy Mission in recent times has rightly shifted to venture into more difficult areas, particularly in the Hindi belt. This has been in recognition of the widening gap in the development process between these States and the remaining States leading to a situation synonymous with an internal colonisation of these States within India and also the fact that the success of the Mission depends on our success in these States where the challenge really lies. In 1993-94, 107 projects were sanctioned under literacy campaigns out of which 53 were in the four Hindi speaking States of Bihar, Madhya Pradesh, Rajasthan and Uttar Pradesh.

10.3.2. Focus on Basis Education

The district literacy project incorporates a plan for enrolling all children in the primary schools and for providing non-formal education to those who drop out from the school system due to various social, economic or other reasons. This group generally constitutes children in the age group of 9-14 years. In addition, District Primary Education Projects are also being taken up in the educationally backward states/areas to provide adequate infrastructure for primary education and to bring about improvement in the quality of schooling so as to enhance participation and reduce dropouts.

10.3.3. Stress on Continuing Education

Education is a continuing process whether it is formal or informal. The NLM is laying stress on consolidation of literacy skills acquired during literacy campaigns in the post literacy and continuing education phase in districts which have completed the literacy campaign phase. The strategy for post literacy and continuing education has been discussed in successive meetings of the Executive Committee of the NLMA.

While undertaking a project, it should be important to know the specificity of the district, achievement levels of learners in the literacy phase, learners' needs and aspirations keeping in view their social and living conditions as well as resources which are available and can be mobilised for the project. Based on the experience gained so far in implementing post literacy projects in different parts of the country, an outline of a strategy for implementation of post literacy and continuing education projects has been endorsed by the NLM.

10.3.4. Equivalency

It is necessary to establish an equivalency level in order to clearly specify the expected levels of learning outcome at the end of the TLC phase. The State Governments are to be advised to establish such equivalency and provide for conducting of examinations to enable the neo-literates to enter the formal education system.

10.4. Features of Literacy Campaigns

10.4.1. Women Participation

India has a tradition to keep its women folk in four walls. Whatever may be the development, the worst affected section will be the women. People are reluctant to send girl child for education. Still the Indians think that educating women are the wastage of money. Women are considered as the machines for reproduction. She gets less education, less food, fewer circumstances to develop.

While implementing adult education, women have invariably been the large majority of participants. Since gender disparity in literacy rates was on an average between 1020% or more, women's participation had to be nearly twice as the participation of men.

The literacy campaigns show that whereas men seem to be more concerned with agriculture, vagaries of unreliable monsoon, power cuts etc than literacy or education, women seem to be extraordinarily resilient, able to absorb miseries of their poverty and yet present themselves with greater hope about the literacy they acquired. They seem to attach pride and happiness about the acquisition of literacy. By and large, women see in the campaigns, a space for themselves in which to interact with each other and to gradually bring about changes in social and more particularly gender equations.

10.4.2. Increasing Demand for Primary Education

There was a great uproar for primary education and enrolment of children in primary schools in many literacy campaign districts. In some districts this has been as a result of conscious efforts of TLC functionaries to arrest the swelling of ranks of illiterates by ensuring attendance of children in schools. In others, this has come about through the realisation of the need and importance of sending children to school. A spurt in demand and enhanced participation in schools have been noticed in those districts where the literacy campaigns have been implemented effectively.

The goal of universalisation of elementary or primary education became a major agenda of the campaign. Many such districts combined the survey of illiterates with a survey of unenrolled children built in and put in sustained efforts for enrolling children in schools as part of the literacy campaign.

10.4.3. Social Concord

The biggest beneficiary of the high rate of literacy is the society. When literacy rate of people in a society increases, the society will also develop. The potential of literacy campaigns to ensure social cohesion is one of the impacts of literacy campaigns noticed in several States and districts. During the height of communal tensions in 1990-92, the campaign areas specially in the village areas did not witness any major communal disturbances. The same is the experience of other districts such as Burdwan in West Bengal, which had a very successful campaign experience. Communally potential incidents were nipped in the bud by the villagers and major potential disturbances averted.

The caste considerations are very important in social equations and interactions. Although teaching-learning takes place in separate groups, some lower caste instructors have taken up teaching work for higher caste illiterate persons or vice-versa. It has also been noticed that caste tensions in such districts at the local level have been substantially reduced.

10.4.4. Support from Administrative Level

The literacy mission will be a failure unless it gets support from administrative level. Quite distinct from the enabling and facilitating role of district and government level functionaries, a large number of TLCs witnessed phenomenal participation from government servants particularly of revenue, development and education departments. In the States of Tamil Nadu, Karnataka and Maharasthra, Gujarat and West Bengal literacy campaigns witnessed the direct involvement of the government set-up in the implementation of the literacy campaigns.

The education department officials including primary and secondary school teachers worked full-time in many of these districts - they not only imparted training to the volunteer teachers but also provided sustained guidance and monitoring. The village literacy committees functioned effectively and where the school teachers' involvement in the literacy campaigns was not under administrative pressure was the improvement in the social accountability of the education system. This was brought about by the coming together and interaction between the primary school teachers, the local community and the village education committee.

10.5. Judging Literacy Campaigns

10.5.1. Self Assessment of learners

The teachers of literacy programmes can check the knowledge of the learners by conducting tests and exercises. This can be done at the end of each lesson in the primers, by which the learner is encouraged to undertake self- evaluation and the instructor and supervisors to understand the progress of learning outcomes.

10.5.2. Internal Assessment of Campaigns

Education is not merely meant by acquiring knowledge. It also influence a person's character. It also evokes punctuality readiness to do the duty. This can be measured by using internal assessments.

10.5.3. External Assessment

By checking the reading, writing and numeric skills of learners, the progress of literacy mission can be evaluated. A learner in order to be successful in the evaluation test should score at least 50% in each of the skills of reading, writing and numeracy and should score 70% in the aggregate. A literacy campaign should succeed in making 80% of the identified learners literate as per the above-mentioned criterion.

10.6. Empowering the Activities of Mission

When people move towards the more difficult and challenging areas in the Hindi speaking states and also to the post literacy and continuing education phase for the higher literacy states, there is need to mobilise the critical and influential opinion makers in the society. Moreover, literacy or educational programmes cannot be implemented in isolation but the society and the community as a whole has to be mobilised. It was decided that in particular, efforts have to be stepped up with the objective of bringing in eminent social scientists, writers, artists, media persons, social activists and others in all possible manner not only to generate an environment supportive of literacy but also to strengthen the resource support for the National Literacy Mission and its various institutions.

10.6.1. Keep Transparency

The Government of India took up the task of monitoring of literacy campaigns seriously from 1993 onwards and streamlined the monitoring of the literacy campaigns under implementation. However, it is not the objective of monitoring of the programmes to merely provide information for financial or programme audit.

The objective of monitoring the programmes has been taken in a much wider sense in the National Literacy Mission in the past one year and the campaigns are also subjected to independent assessments/scrutiny by people from different walks of life and sections of society. The periodical reports and returns that are brought out by evaluating agencies or Joint Evaluation Teams are not the only mechanism of monitoring the programmes. They are supplemented by visits to the campaigns by consultants to the National Literacy Mission, other non- officials, media persons, social activists etc.

10.7. Practices of Monitoring and Evaluation

The evaluation of is inevitable for the smooth functioning of a programme. The practices of monitoring and evaluation (M&E practices) at the national level consist of the following:

10.7.1. Pre-Evaluation

Before implementing a programme, it must be well evaluated. The pre evaluation will help to find out correct the problems which may arise while undertaking that project. Every literacy campaign project proposal, when formulated by a duly constituted district literacy committee, is pre-appraised by a team of Consultants of the NLMA who are generally outsiders to the programme. The NLMA has laid down certain acceptable criteria by which to assess the extent of preparedness of a district/ project to take up a campaign.

The project can be evaluated by doing survey, training, distribution of primers, progress of teaching-learning, achievement of learning outcomes, expenditure of funds and also the outcome of the campaign. The focus of monitoring is on achievement of learning outcomes which is facilitated by the standardised graded set of three primers representing three distinct levels of achievement. The achievement levels are, therefore, monitored. Evaluation focuses primarily on the various inputs, processes and outcomes. But the literacy campaigns are regularly encouraged and exhorted to report qualitatively on the strengths and weaknesses of the campaigns as well as the highlights of achievements particularly focusing on functionality and awareness aspects.

10.7.2. Spot Evaluations

Spot evaluation is also needed for the successful implementation of literacy mission activities. For time to time, the top officials visit districts/projects which do not show satisfactory, performance. This is a process of management by exception taking up those districts on priority which appear to lag behind. Such visits are in the nature of spot evaluations at selected representative spots in the district/ campaign area including a qualitative first hand study on the quality of survey, environment building, training, teaching-learning, progress of teaching-learning etc coupled with discussions at village, community development, block and district levels with officials and non-officials of the respective committees. Based on such extensive feedback, the reports generated are disseminated and programme implementation is sought to be improved.

The periodical and regular review meetings become interesting feedback-cum-orientation sessions to strengthen the implementation of the campaigns. A process of review and discussion on a regular basis has now been initiated at the level of chief ministers of states, particularly the four major Hindi-speaking States.

10.8. Drawbacks of National Literacy Mission

The National Literacy Mission was a success. But it doesn't mean that the mission was free from drawbacks. The serious weaknesses of the programme are:

(i) The main objective of the Literacy Mission was 'totaol literacy.' But there has been significant fudging/ overestimation of achievement figures in districts where TLCs have been launched and completed or near-completed. The pressures leading to such overestimation are not just the result of bad intentions but also of good intentions related to the 'movement' character of the TLC.

(ii) The real fragility in literacy achievements was very serious problems of relapse of neo-literates even in districts where there have been successful TLCs. This problem is aggravated in cases of long time lags between TLC & PL/ CE.

(iii) Literacy has become a relatively high profile issue. But large and easily accessible funds are available for sanctioning TLC projects. More district collectors and administrative officials view the TLC only as a career enhancing scheme. There is considerable pressure to meet 'politically committed' targets i.e. full literacy by the year 2000 - the over- all result is the emergence of a strong tendency to both press for, and to sanction, TLC projects even in areas where there is inadequate preparation, sometimes no preparation except on paper. The consequences of such sanctions are extremely detrimental, indeed counter productive. There is grave danger that the credibility of a good programme will be fatally jeopardised if such pressures are not resisted.

(iv) The people-oriented approach is tending to be replaced by bureaucrats alone, both with respect to project formulation and with respect to implementation. This malaise is particularly in evidence in some of the Hindi speaking states, and even in others where people's mobilisation had been high earlier. This is a major cause of the declining tempo of the ' movement' and for greater volunteer fatigue.

(v) The Hindi heartland states constitute the area where the problem of adult illiteracy is most acute. And here there are serious specific problems large size of illiterates; relatively small size of the pool of literates from which volunteer instructors are to be drawn, with most literates residing in urban areas; lack of recent literacy tradition/movements in these states; widening gender bias against women visible in all indicators, including literacy; low political commitment to the eradication of illiteracy; diverse socio-political, caste and communal tensions.

10.9. Conclusion

In India, education was considered as birth right of the upper class. Even today, some regions in India follows this custom and the backward communities are still kept far away from acquiring knowledge. A generation acquires development only through education. Realising this fact, the government of India has been adopting a number of methods to educate her people. But, the lack of commitments to continue these programmes, most of these are in a state of standstill. Adult education must be an endless process.

References

Panicker, P. N., "KANFED - a private organization promoting adult education", Adult Education and Development, no. 15, 1980.

Reghu, V., "Preparation of books for neo-literates in post-literacy and continuing education programmes (India)", Adult Education and Development, 1999.

Tharakan, P K Michael, "Ernakulam re-visited: a study of literacy in the first totally literate District in India", in M. Karlekar (ed), *Reading the World: Understanding the literacy campaigns in India*, Bombay: Asia South Pacific Bureau of Adult Education, 2000.

11

Continuing Education and Lifelong Learning

11.1. Introduction

Learning is a continuous process and it should not end in school or collage level. Instead, it continues still the student become a proficient in his/her respective field. This process of update is known as continuous education. Continuing education, professional development and lifelong learning are all terms used to describe an educational or training process that is a key component for successful organisations. In this process, a person need not attend school on a regular full-time basis.

In the primitive stages of human development, education was not so much important because people depend entirely on agricultural or physical activities for living. With the growth of population and the development of industrialised economy, education became the sole determinant for getting an enviable job. Besides, several environmental factors also are driving the demand for lifelong learning in the twenty-first century: abundant access to information, rapid technology changes, increased global interactions, industry shifts, as well as increasing entry level credentials and skill requirements.

The employment scenario also has undergone tremendous changes and for hiring highly skilled and qualified workforce, employers also depend on continuing education. Individuals use continuing education for upward career mobility, job enhancement and personal enrichment.

11.2. Continuing Education

The continuous education process is not bound by time and place. In other words, it can be done in any where or any time. The format for the continuing education learning should be driven by the content and learning goals. Internet and satellite technology allow employees to engage in educational coursework on the job or at home, which results in a tremendous savings of travel costs and time. Continuing education courses are offered for academic or university level credit, as well as non-credit courses. Many organisations take advantage of "off-the shelf" or commission for customised content that is offered through their own employee training group.

Today, education has a vital part in everybody's life and must always have continuity. It should not be aborted before completion. It is not normally considered to include basic instruction such as literacy, English language skills, or programmes such as vocational training or GED preparation. Instead, the student already has an education and is simply continuing it.

Professional continuing education is a specific learning activity generally characterised by the issuance of a certificate or Continuing Education Units (CEU) for the purpose of documenting attendance at a designated seminar or course of instruction. Licensing bodies in a number of fields impose continuing education requirements on members who hold licenses to practice within a particular profession. These requirements are intended to encourage professionals to expand their knowledge base and stay up-to-date on new developments. Depending on the field, these requirements may be satisfied through college or university coursework, extension courses or conferences and seminars attendance.

11.3. Lifelong Learning

Learning is an endless. The entire life of a person, from the cradle to grave, is an institute for acquiring knowledge. This is the basic principle of lifelong learning. Throughout the last decade the concept of life-long learning has continued to gain popularity. Organisations in the twenty-first century are challenged to quickly adapt to industry changes and rapidly identify solutions for obstacles or barriers that the organisation encounters. Through the lifelong learning process, individuals develop the capacity for addressing this organisational need. Key characteristics of lifelong learning include duration, learner-centered perspective, multi-level and multi-subject learning, and open access.

The process of lifelong learning gives emphasis on learner rather than instructor or trainer. Obviously, an instructor is inevitable for acquiring knowledge. But at the same, he/she must be skilled at providing an educational environment that allows the individual to enhance and engage in his or her own learning objectives. The learning format and content should be designed with the learner in mind.

Lifelong learners require choices and educational experiences that fit within their lifestyle. The educational activity should balance the needs and convenience of the organisation with individual learner's need in order to maximise the learning outcome. Lifelong learning activities are also designed for multiple learning styles. Experiential and applied learning as well as tutorials and self-directed content are often embraced by lifelong learners.

Skill training, credential requirements, as well as social interests are the major areas of lifelong learning. This education may be in the form of formal education or training that is offered both as credit and non-credit in a variety of venues. It also occurs through non-formal means such as libraries, museums, manuals and mentors.

In lifelong learning, any individual can acquire knowledge irrespective of age, race, ability, prior qualifications, workplace role or socio demographics. Innovative delivery formats help to ensure that the learning activities are accessible to anyone that is interested in participating.

11.3.1. Significance of Lifelong Learning

11.3.1.1. Method of Learning from Life

Lifelong learning is getting popularity day by day. The reasons behind growing interest in education are mounting pressures for providing individualised, non-traditional, or distance learning opportunities, and available evidence that formal school experience does not adequately equip people to cope with life's challenges.

The rapidity and constancy of change is one of the major forces act in concert to generate the interest for lifelong learning. There are some components of change, some of them fundamental in nature that has impacted adults in various ways to specifically cause an increased need for learning.

People should learn to act positively with the rapid changes, technological developments, and constant concerns about future inflation. Continuous change requires continuous learning. Unfortunately, there exist in society many adults unable or unwilling to change, to learn, or to manage their own lives satisfactorily-adults who frequently are led to believe that a better life awaits if only more and more of the material things produced by technological change can be obtained.

As per the structure and patter of normal schooling, the learners-especially the poor, the disadvantaged, and the ethnic minority-were inadequately prepared to cope with most of the main societal problems they faced. The results they believed were dysfunctionally schooled products who relied on further institutionalised education for problem solving rather than self-directed or self-motivated learners who knew how to avail themselves of a variety of resources, both personal and external, to cope with various problems.

Finding a proper income source is a must for every people. Occupational half-life is based on the assumption that enough new developments, techniques, and/or knowledge evolve in a short period of time, say 5-15 years, so that a person becomes roughly half as competent to do the job for which his or her initial training was intended. Consequently, adults frequently must turn to learning activities in and out of the workplace just to maintain or regain competence.

The life style of the people has also changed a lot. Now, none of us are interested to work on 24 hour basis. Instead, everybody likes to leisure in between. A movement toward self-actualisation or the many concerns for saving or improving the environment, more and more people believe that a full and rich life is possible primarily through the maximisation of individual potentiality. Consequently, an increasing attention toward interpersonal communication skills, values clarification, and self-identity activities is becoming very recognisable in people's learning efforts.

For leading a decent life, education is inevitable. However, to enhance the development of people's potential, many of the basic attitudes and skills possessed by educators toward learners and the learning process must change. The idea of dispensing pre-established knowledge to a vacuum in the form of a student will need to be supplemented by, and in many instances exchanged for, a cooperative relationship between the learner and teacher in a mutual process of problem solving, self-discovery, and just plain learning how to learn.

11.3.1.2. *Revolutionary Learning Methods*

Education is meant for both learning and solving problems in life. But many adults have resisted participating in, or after a short sampling have dropped out of, traditional learning activities. At the same time, there exists much interest in learning by adults and an apparently high participation in learning endeavours outside normal institutional forms of education.

Education professionals have begun to pay particular attention to non-traditional forms for, and delivery systems of, learning. Non-traditional activities, alternative learning modes, or innovative educational changes are based primarily on the assumption that lifelong learning is a natural circumstance of life within which autonomous, self-directed learners participate according to their needs and interests. More change can be expected and must happen if education is to meet a goal of truly helping people with a lifetime of challenges.

11.3.1.3. *Hurdles before Teachers of Adults*

Even though, the lifelong learning is not bound by time, proper updates in the curriculum is needed for getting best results. Curriculum updating is frequently geared to content changes with new information; attention is seldom given to finding ways of incorporating curriculum with the challenges that occur throughout a lifetime. Unless students at undergraduate or graduate levels are directly involved with curriculum designed to build teachers or trainers of adults, frequently they are taught that the school is an island to which people come for a predetermined amount of time, rather than viewing the school as one resource in an educative environment.

Advanced learning credentials possessed by individuals do not automatically signal all is well in life. National achievement test scores are decreasing over time, numerous doctoral degree holders are unable to find meaningful work, and school systems have been sued by students or parents who claim viable forms of education are not received. The number of school dropouts is increasing day by day. When the dropout rates increases, the eventual price such individuals must pay can be enormous. Moreover, today's student often has a poor attitude about school and learning. As a result, teachers and trainers of adults often are faced with students inadequately prepared for advanced education.

The teachers of the adult students must think of themselves more as educators, instead of fairly narrow specialists such as high school science teachers, junior high counsellors, or elementary school principals, if learning is to become lifelong instead of something that is discontinued at age 16, 18, or 22. In many respects the role of the teacher in such learning settings must change to that of facilitating student learning, helping such students learn to use the many resources now available electronically, and promoting in learners attitudes of and commitment to lifelong learning.

However, there are many differing views regarding the role of the teacher in a learning setting. Perhaps the most widely accepted view is that the teacher is one who imparts knowledge on a subject to others. Indeed, teacher training efforts frequently involve the development of content specialisation by a teacher and, concurrently, the provision of training in various techniques, methods, and devices so that the person will become skillful in presenting any knowledge inherent in the specialisation.

The lifelong learning programme possesses some potential weaknesses also. If a receptor does not want to receive some predetermined knowledge because she or he is tired, fearful of the whole learning endeavour, or interested in something else-as can happen with adult learners of varying ages-then it is very difficult to simply impart some knowledge. Every one has different viewpoints. What a teacher might perceive as the important point on some topic might be perceived quite differently by the learner. Consequently, teacher training efforts must be aimed at more than the development of information transmittal skills.

For providing better awareness to the adult learners, the teachers need to become more skilled. For this, more attention be given to a discipline of learning where the rigor of analysis and the capacity to acquire new knowledge as needed are addressed foremost in the learning setting. The teachers must be able to help learners determine their needs, discover what resources can be brought to bear on these needs, and match the resources with the needs. Learning in this type of arrangement becomes one of integrating the educational process with life's activities.

Teachers are the active partners of the adult students in the educational process. So, teachers must realise that each student has a potential and various experiences. This factor moves the instructional process toward one of a cooperative student-teacher relationship, with the teacher as a facilitative resource person and the learner as an autonomous seeker of necessary knowledge. Such an ideal relationship is not obtained easily; however, it is something possible, particularly as both the learner and instructor become confident in the process.

Teachers must be learning process consultants for adult learners and the school, classroom, and community must be the learning resource centers. In addition, this instructional approach requires the skills to promote self-inquiry, to involve students and others in programme or course planning, and to facilitate individualised learning activities.

Teaching aptitudes improve when teachers try to teach self-inquiry skills, individualisation of instruction, team teaching, and the open or on-line classroom. Indeed, it is expected that the movement toward creating lifelong learning skills will provide opportunities for teachers and trainers to improve or to shift their teaching styles and for the trainers of trainers or teachers to do even better jobs.

If all teachers or trainers are to become effective in the facilitation of lifelong learning and in the utilisation of a variety of innovative approaches to teaching or learning, they must come to grips with the concept of education as a lifetime process and need.

Teachers must be ready to help their students at each stages of learning. They must be aware about how to use agency or individual expertise as supplemental and primary learning resources, how to help learners use community resources in solving problems, and how to develop curricula that help learners understand the relationships between subject matter and later or emerging lives in the community. These changes require that educators in training be exposed to community theory, be able to work closely with community leaders, be exposed to the community through various activities, and be involved in studying communities and their resources through community survey techniques.

The educators must possess excellent skills for giving job retraining to the learners. Because so many people who eventually work with educational programmes for adults arrive in such positions by accident rather than by design, it is suggested that teacher preparation institutions and those working with the training of trainers-especially those that attempt to incorporate the concept of educator as a lifelong learning facilitator--need to consider the various types of clientele who will be recipients of educational efforts.

However, the changes cannot be accomplished overnight. Attitudes will need to change, innovations will need to be tried and tested, and new teaching or training strategies will need to be discovered. Hopefully, however, those responsible for the training of trainers and educators are beginning to meet such challenges with new and experimental approaches to their preparation efforts.

11.3.2. Difficulties in Lifelong Learning

For the successful implementation of lifelong learning needs the correction of several plaguing problems. Educational philosophers, leaders, and practitioners will need to find the solutions.

i) Much greater precision is needed in defining what are inquiry skills or lifelong learning skills, what bearing, if any, age has on such skills, and how such skills might be taught.

ii) In a lifelong learning environment, what will be the role of educational institutions and what will be the differences, if any, between techniques used by individuals working with children and those used in working with adults?

iii) The concept of community (i.e., boundaries, roles, power structures, etc) will require change to accommodate a lifelong learning environment.

iv) How will the evolving "for profit" educational programmes affect the lifelong learning movement?

v) The two or three generations of individuals caught between a traditional education structure and a lifelong learning society will need to be given special attention.

vi) The role of higher education in a lifelong learning environment will need to be examined.

11.3.3. Responsibility of the Parents

Children are totally dependable to their parents for each of their needs. Basic needs of food, shelter, safety, and love are fulfilled primarily by parents in the home environment. In addition, in the early years of life a person is taught values, learns what is expected of self and others, and has individual abilities fostered.

It is the prime responsibility of parents to nurture their children with intellectual development. In addition to playing a role in stimulating intellectual growth, parents are also important ingredients in the development of a child's physical, social, and emotional growth. The first few years of life are extremely important; later success in life is often related to the roles parents played in that early life and to the type of attitudes toward education and lifelong learning that were nurtured in the home.

Education through the school setting is, of course, extremely important, but there must be a link between what transpires in the home in terms of intellectual development or attitudes toward learning and what exists in the classroom. Adult educators can play an important role in helping to link the family and the school.

Without the cooperation of adults in a community, education and stimulation of youth degrade merely a dream. The parents have the responsibility to create a learning environment in the home. It should be continued with school officials and parents cooperating on educational pursuits by children in and out of the home, and is supplemented by adult educators continually facilitating growth through parent education programmes and other lifelong learning opportunities.

There are a variety of educational programmes designed for parents also. Adult educators need to establish educational opportunities within which parents can learn more about the community and its many resources available to supplement the intellectual and physical development of the child from birth to adulthood. Such educational activities would be especially important when the child is of preschool age because so much is learned and most attitudes about learning are formed before a person ever enters the formal classroom. Many such opportunities become continuing education for parents and can fill a variety of educational needs not already being met through existing programs or institutions.

11.3.4. Role of the Society in Adult Education

The society has a very important role in educating the adults. The various community activities suggested and the many others possible for families will be effective in stimulating learning only if they are made effective by knowledgeable parents and integrated with what is taking place when a child enters a classroom. Thus, the adult and continuing educator must work closely with both the parent and the educator.

The society is changing rapidly and every citizen gain new skills, new understandings, and new intellectual orientations throughout his life in order to live satisfactorily. Formal education confined to the first two decades or so of a person's life cannot possibly prepare one for the constancy and rapidity of change, lifelong learning becomes an imperative if each person is to cope with the explosion of knowledge, understand societal differences as they evolve, and adapt to the aging process. Thus, adult educators must help people keep their learning skills sharp and provide the best possible facilitative environment for learning.

The nature of work also varies in due course and many people face several different careers in a lifetime because of changing interests or certain occupations coming obsolete. In addition, many professionals such as those in medical health areas must constantly study and learn if they are to remain proficient. Adult educators have a tremendous responsibility in facilitating occupational training and education for the professionals.

People fail to cope up with the changing nature of society because of the inadequacy of education or training. In reality, each state has a large number of individuals with virtually no education at all, and, as indicated earlier, school dropout rates are increasing and in some states the average level of education has dropped in the past few years. Although increased education does not automatically mean a better life nor is education a panacea to cure all social ills, the adult educator has an important role to play in improving the literacy of many people.

Local problems can be solved by involving in community action or community development projects, and simply being confident in communicating with others are important personal activities. Thus, a variety of life skills are required if societal ills disliked by so many are to be cured. People can effectively use their leisure time for meaningful activities and learning pursuits designed for personal growth throughout a lifetime.

11.4. Barriers in Adult and Continuing Education

The society has immense responsibility in adult and continuing education. However, there are several obstacles that have prevented and are continuing to prevent lifelong learning from becoming a reality for all individuals.

Although the popularity of adult education as a field of study or as a profession is spreading very slowly, this situation may change due to the worldwide interest in lifelong learning. Many need critically for new knowledge, and the actual increasing involvement of adults in various kinds of adult education or training activities. This marginal status has created difficulties for adult education in achieving local, state, and federal financial support and, to a certain extent, in working with other educational professionals.

The educational set of every country focus on youth. Even in a few decades back, if a person possesses certain amount of knowledge and any resulting skills by the magical age of 16, 18, or 22, he/she will be prepared for life. Learning is indeed lifelong and that learning skills and positive attitudes toward continuous learning are extremely important goals for educational efforts aimed at a youth population.

The adult educators also face problems such as the fear of, or dislike for, school that preoccupies many people. Because of failures in early schooling, dissatisfaction with certain teachers or subjects, and the expectation that adult education simply will be an extension of earlier education, the adult educator often has difficulty in recruiting certain individuals into educational programs. Such a situation should change as the idea of lifelong learning becomes more widespread and as educators become more skilled at facilitating learning activities in other than the traditional classroom setting.

11.4.1. Prerequisites for a Trainer of Adults

The scenario of adult and continuing education is widening and the adults are thinking seriously about this matter. So, the teachers and administrators who work or will work primarily in adult education programmes should not belittle the importance of such activities. The teachers must help the adult students understand the need for lifelong learning and perhaps even encouraging parents to utilise adult education as a means for personal growth.

Continue education throughout life is the development of love for learning and numerous corresponding tools for learning. Such tools would include self-inquiry skills, the ability to undertake independent study, a curiosity about life, and knowledge regarding how to utilise a variety of resources for learning that exist inside of the normal classroom. Adult educators must deal with the factors such as the impact of the parent and family environment in the early years, the ability of the parent to supplement at home education that takes place in the school, and the attitude about education and learning that parents transmit to their children. Consequently, adult educators encourage to utilise adult and continuing education opportunities for their own personal growth and improvement as parents.

Education provides extra mileage to the growth of a person. A new educational lifestyle is indeed emerging one in which learning is being looked to not only for vocational reasons but also for personal growth reasons. Educators at all levels have a crucial role to play in assisting with such an evolution and helping to bring about a society based on lifelong learning.

11.4.2. Topics of Adult Learners

The adult learners are the hapless people who are thrown out of the mainstream learning process due to adverse circumstances. In an adult stage, they all are looking for getting a decent life from education. So, the topics for them must be selected accordingly. In several parts of the country, colleges and universities are either struggling to maintain enrollments or have needed to institute new programs. These types of changes, fewer educational investment dollars, demands for service from special groups such as the elderly and the poor, and workplace training needs have worked in concert to help educators "re-discover" the adult client.

Even though, many nations have a high literacy rate, adult learning needs are also very high.. In addition, the poverty of millions, coping needs of many resulting from an aging population, access problems experienced by adults with disabilities, and frequent job retraining or upgrading needs are constant reminders that educators and trainers of adults still have many challenges ahead of them.

11.4.3. Uniqueness of the Adult Learner

To describe an adult learner in specific terms is impossible. There are almost as many different learning styles, needs, and rates of involvement as there are adults. It can certainly be said that every adult has the capability and potential for engaging in learning activities.

There are probably many more adults engaged in education and learning than has ever been tabulated by census bureaus and other agencies who identify educational enrollment numbers. Many educators are beginning to pay attention not only to the uniqueness of the adult learner in terms of learning styles, but also to the tremendous interest in, and need for, self directed, individual learning.

Adults are unique individuals and they have many personal responsibilities to fulfill as members of society or as helpers or providers to others. This encompasses the need for learning as liberal education, in developing oneself to cope as best as possible with the continual problems that plague humans, as a functional vehicle for providing some meaning or bringing some joy to life, and in providing vocational/occupational skills.

The individuality of an adult learner also extends to the actual conduct of most learning activities. The growing body of knowledge and research central to adult and continuing education is replete with evidence of the adult's many unique characteristics, needs, and learning styles. The first and, perhaps, most important characteristic deals with the self-concept of the adult. For most, to be adult means to be independent, to possess a certain amount of self-motivation, and to be capable of making decisions about life and its problems.

Another unique characteristic of an adult learner is the wide and varied accumulation of experience with life that each adult possesses. A person engaging in a learning activity does not do so with this experience slate wiped clean. Consequently, the type and amount of educational need will vary, as will each person's desire or ability to bring this experience to bear upon the learning endeavour.

Every adult has a variety of problems or limitations that contribute to individual uniqueness. Just the simple variable of age will impinge on each person differently in terms of visual or hearing acuteness, learning ability, and the energy level required for engaging in learning. In addition, the problems of life that one faces do not disappear when engaging in an educational endeavour and will undoubtedly affect such learning factors as retention, interest, and comprehension ability.

The fear of the new, uncertainty of pushing back boundaries, and remembrance of past learning failures or unsatisfactory experiences also can affect the adult engaged in learning. Learning is a lifelong pursuit and a necessity will take place on very much an individual timetable.

Understanding the uniqueness of the adult learner is a necessary requirement for effectiveness with the teaching/learning process or in developing educational resources. Educators must reckon with the freedom and dignity of each person in society. This is based on the premise that each individual needs to be free to realise personal potential and that the success of a society is predicated on the interdependence of all its members. Consequently, a teaching and learning process for adults must be built to respond to the unique needs of those engaged in it.

11.4.4. Categories of Adult Learners

Adult learners can be categorised into different ways, although no one category is mutually exclusive or all-encompassing. However, the purpose of suggesting some differences as to why people engage in learning is to highlight some implications for the entire teaching-learning process.

People are undergoing adult learning programmes for various reasons and they can be categorised accordingly. Within each category there will no doubt be differences based on such variables as age, sex, level of educational attainment, and other similar characteristics. However, the categories provide a means for understanding something about the nature and actions of those people who actively engage in formal learning activities. A fourth category is added to reflect current research findings on learning outside of formal opportunities.

11.4.4.1. Goal-Oriented

The learners are going for learning activities for fulfilling certain goals. Such a goal might be the desire to obtain a driver's license, a high school diploma, or a college degree. Very often such goals are related to one's occupation. The point is that the learner can justify or tie each learning endeavour to a distinct purpose felt necessary or important.

11.4.4.2. Activity-Oriented

Some people join adult learning courses for their desire to involve in activity oriented programmes. Because of loneliness, because of a boring day, because of wanting to be with others, or various other similar reasons, certain people seem to thrive on social contact or involvement.

11.4.4.3. Learning-Oriented

People are different in nature. Some enjoy learning for their own sake, they typically read a lot, they make use of the community library, the museum, the Internet, or other, similar resources, and they often seem to have an interest in a never-ending number of subjects.

11.4.4.4. Self-Directed Learner

The self-directed learner is not always fully recognised or easily recognisable. The self-reliant, autonomous, and independent learner now has the attention of adult education professionals.

Learners move through each category, depending upon their needs, their stage of development, or the availability of learning resources. In addition, it is just as probable that many more categories will emerge as the learner becomes better understood.

11.4.5. Menace of Undereducated Adults

The development of a nation depends on the literacy rate of the people of that country. The increasing number of undereducated people is a menace to the society. The undereducated fail to obtain a decent job and it will ultimately affect the economic foundation of the nation. In a society that can build a space station that sees billions spent each year on entertainment, and that can produce consumer goods at a rate considerably higher than elsewhere in the world, the educational deficiencies are difficult to understand.

Educated people are capable to change their profession according to the changes in the society. Many community members also face problems of job obsolescence, unemployment or layoffs, and low paying jobs where attaining a living wage is very difficult. Add to this the continuing problem of school dropout, violence among young people, and a growing number of elderly poor and alarm bells need to go off for caring individuals.

Resources are unlimited. But the people who are going to tap these resources must be to utilise it fully. The opportunities for the educational field, and for educators and trainers of adults are immense and such opportunities will not be overlooked.

11.4.6. Problems of the Older Adults

As poverty is the main obstacle on the path of formal education, it also appears before the people in their old age. Many of the elderly are subjected to inadequate housing, poor nutrition, and substandard health care due to a low and usually fixed income level. An unexpected and prolonged heat wave in a large urban area may result in the death of several older people. Fear of violence in the streets or even in stairwells keeps many older people away for the very educational or training programs that could help them in various ways.

The older person also faces various cognitive inhibitors to learning. Although there are many individual differences, some elderly people face declining memory potential, a slowing of conditional responses, and difficulties in sorting out learning that is based on long, sequentially related tasks. Some potential psychological limitations are lack of interest, fear of learning, and negative self-concepts.

Whatever may be the hindrance, the older person has a tremendous, mostly untapped, potential for learning. Community colleges, other institutions of higher education, and many community organisations are beginning to offer special programmes for senior citizens with considerable success in terms of the numbers enrolling. The older person is willing to be an active learner and become even more active as opportunities are made available can be shown when their involvement in learning outside of institutionally sponsored programmes is examined.

People in old age are very interested for learning. They have a need, yearning, and potential for active participation in lifelong learning. Strides are being made to help the elderly become full partners in educational activity. Hopefully, the educational field will continue to make available to people of all ages increasing opportunities and resources for learning.

11.5. Role of Adult Educators

The adult education programmes open a wide opportunity for those who dropped out of the mainstream education. So, there are various types of roles performed by individuals who consider themselves to be professional adult educators. The variety of roles is increasing as the profession matures. However, there appear to be three fairly distinct categories or types.

11.5.1. Administrative Roles

Adult education programmes are conducted outside the framework of educational institutions. So, administrative role is very significant in organising and implementing adult education efforts. Whether it is a community college, a learning resource center, a YMCA, or a voluntary agency, someone must administer the programmes, be in charge of teacher and student recruitment, work with the board or council, develop a suitable budget, and give the basic programme leadership.

Adult education is often in a marginal or supporting role, with scarce resources, an evolving "territory," and an ever-changing clientele base. In addition, adult participants seldom are enrolled in educational programs unless they want to be. This means, therefore, that the adult education administrator must thoroughly understand how to involve the adult student in the learning endeavour, design programmes based on adult needs, and set up learning activities that are based on what is known about how adults learn. Such an understanding must be the basis for programme planning, training teachers, and coordinating each single effort with a workable whole.

11.5.2. Teaching Roles

The main syllabus in an adult education programme is how to face the problems in life. So, the position of a teacher or trainer ranges from full-time adult basic education teachers, to teachers of noncredit evening classes such as quilting, oil painting, or wills and estate planning, to vocational teachers in a trade or proprietary school, to trainer in a large company. However, many adult education teachers do not earn their primary incomes in such roles.

The field of adult education is in an evolving stage compared to most other professions, probably the largest share of adult education teachers or trainers have had very little specific training related to the adult as learner. Hopefully, as the field matures, as it gains better financial support, and as adult teacher-training programmes are more fully developed, this situation can be reversed.

11.5.3. Professorial Roles

An adult educator must be ready for dividing their time between (a) teaching and working with students who are wanting to become adult educators or to become at least acquainted with the field, (b) carrying out research and scholarly pursuits related to adult education as a profession, and (c) carrying out a variety of service activities that attempt to extend the resources of the department and university beyond the campus walls.

11.5.4. Miscellaneous Roles

The adult educators are also act as counsellors for their students. The role of learning resource center facilitator needs teaching skills, counselling skills, and administrative skills; however, they also need to be skilled at directing individualised learning, discovering various resources for learning outside the normal classroom setting, establishing technology-based learning efforts, and coordinating the learning efforts of several learners progressing at various rates.

The adult educators can be mentors who work with learners primarily on a one-to-one basis, on-line teachers who use computer mediated communication techniques, or instructional designers who develop individualised learning materials. Such individuals must serve as teachers, helpers, designers, and advisors, as well as being a contributor to program-planning effort and a developer of learning resources. Such a person not only needs to thoroughly understand how to work with the adult learner, but also how to discover and coordinate a variety of resources for learning that are available in most communities or through electronic means.

There is a fairly recognisable pattern to the nature of training received in adult education. One or more courses built around each of the following competency expectations usually serve as a base for the training effort:

- Understanding learning theory as it applies to the adult.
- Understanding the adult personality and adult psychology.
- Skill in administering adult education programming efforts.
- Skill in planning and evaluating adult education programs.
- Knowledge of technology, especially as it impacts on or supports adult learning.
- Understanding emerging and evolving theory that is related specifically to adult education.

— Knowledge of the various philosophical adult education underpinnings.

— Knowledge of the history of adult education in the United States.

— Understanding the institutions and forms of adult education.

— Knowledge of the societal issues important to adult education.

— Ability to carry out research in adult education.

The expectations of doctoral degree will be greater than bachelors or masters degree requirements. Such expectations usually include greater exposure to the behavioural sciences through course work outside of adult education, practical experience in adult education through internships or practicum, and demonstrations of scholarly abilities through advanced research-related course work, independent research activities, and published materials.

11.5.5. In-Service Training

Many people find themselves carrying out responsibilities related to working with adults almost accidentally. So, in-service training related to the education of adults serves an important role. Consequently, many individuals increase their skills and knowledge through a variety of in-service means.

Short term workshops are the very common means of obtaining help in working with the adult learner. Often for two or three weeks and sometimes for graduate credit, these workshops provide a concentrated exposure to some aspect of adult education. The largest share of such workshops is usually concentrated on the improvement of skills, such as in selecting appropriate methods and materials for the adult learner, designing instructional settings for adults, and developing more effective communication skills in working with the independently inclined adult person.

Seminars or conferences are another often-used means of providing training. The typical time allotment is even shorter than for workshops, usually two or three days. The purpose is often to provide new information or to heighten awareness on such topics as the uniqueness of the adult learner, research findings related to adult education, and new approaches in adult education.

11.5.6. Implications

To provide graduate or in-service training as well as the retraining and upgrading of individuals who have responsibilities in adult and continuing education programmes, many additional means is also be required. The shortage of trained adult educators is still a reality, despite the various graduate program opportunities. In addition, research efforts in adult education are continuously providing new information that needs to be disseminated to continuing education professionals in a variety of ways.

The adult educators must be skilled at solving various kinds of problems, especially the many problems that emerge because of growth and societal change. Adult education leaders frequently will need to be more social-action or change-agent oriented if they are to help adults become better equipped to solve various societal problems. Finally, educators and trainers of adults must become technologically adept to ensure the programmes they offer meet the needs and expectations of learners.

11.6. Role of Community in Adult and Continuing Education

The community has an important role in conducting adult and continuing education programmes. Thus, it is important to facilitate an understanding of the concept of community and its relationship to people so that future problem solving through education may be made more effective.

11.6.1. Knowing Community

Human beings are social animals. So, the community they belong to has a major role in the development of a person. People need support and encouragement from community for their growth. The term community refers to a geographical unit of people organised in such a manner that the fulfillment of normal, daily living needs is met. For many people such needs are fulfilled in the neighbourhood or small town setting. However, some people would say that their natural home base was a large urban center and this would be their community setting.

Most individuals have two different kinds of pulls on them that affect their relationship to others regardless of the actual setting or size of a community. One kind of pull is vertical in nature. By that it is meant that a person might live in Buffalo, New York, but have affiliatory relationships to organisations, associations, and individuals outside the community that tend to draw allegiances, time of residence, and resources away from where they live.

The second kind of pull or relationship is horizontal in nature, or within the community. In other words, most people are affiliated with many people, groups, and organisations in the same community where they live.

Due to advancing technology and constant social change, the dynamic state of modern society is continuously imposing new strains on daily living. One may hold a personal value judgment on whether constant change is good or bad, but the vertical pulls are becoming increasingly more apparent as we are urged to become a world society. Adult education as a vital force in lifelong learning can be a means of strengthening the horizontal relationships of a people within their own communities and thereby facilitate a heightened sense of community.

The relationship of community to education for adults is fairly direct. People are primarily the product of a community in which they were born and/or raised. Some people receive vocational retraining, for example, as the local job conditions demand it. Many college graduates return to their local communities, even if after living elsewhere for several years. In addition, educational access often gained through local channels of communication. Thus, adult education programs and activities are carried out in local schools or community colleges, through local agencies or organisations, in the training rooms of local companies, and by using forms of media with which the person is acquainted.

The local community is a logical setting for adult and continuing education that is aimed at helping people fulfill citizenship roles and solve their own unique community problems.

11.6.2. Community Education Movement

Education is the scale of a nation's development. Each year, the government implements a lot of developmental activities in the state. For chanalising those activities in a fruitful way, people must be literate. The community has a very important role for educating its people. Perhaps even more important is the potential that community education has in involving adults with educational activities.

The community education movement has received important contributions from a variety of institutions, agencies, and community centers in addition to those of the public schools and the cooperating universities. Perhaps one of the most important of these institutions has been the community and junior college. Through the community service programmes, the colleges provide various kinds of adult education programmes, coordinate community education programmes, and generally attempt to meet the educational needs of citizens not already met through other college or public school programmes.

11.6.3. Need of Community Development

The large number of educated adults in a community shows the development. Community development can be defined as the educational facilitation of an interaction between a community and its residents for purposes of an improvement of both. Thus, dealing with change in any community, the solution of crucial community problems, and the corresponding development of leadership are results of the community development process that go beyond what typically is a part of community education.

Community development activities can be undertaken effectively by implementing the community education movement. The involvement of the community resident in a solution of problems is a crucial aspect within the adult educator's view of the community development process.

11.6.4. Role of Educators and Trainers

Educators and trainers of adults can and usually do play an important role in the community setting. Whether it is from an institutional or agency base or as a private individual, the skills possessed by adult educators and trainers can be used in many important ways. By working with the adults, the educators understand people and their problems. Thus, the assessment of needs through community surveys or studies, through advisory councils, by personal observation, by discussions with community leaders, and through a multitude of other techniques is a necessary element in the development of adult and continuing education programmes or the facilitation of a community development project.

The adult educator has a responsibility to establish a teaching and learning climate that will maximise the learning and involvement that takes place. Such a process includes facilitating the needs-assessment activities described above, making available various resources for learning, utilising a person's community experiences as a basis for learning, and providing facilitating expertise as it is necessary.

The various agencies and organisations sponsoring educational programmes prevent overlap, that needless competition can be minimised, and the use of resources can be maximised. Thus, the adult educator or trainer has an important role to play in coordinating such activities as the use of expensive educational buildings, in determining what audiences can be served best by each agency, by ascertaining the educational and training areas of highest priority, and by making information on educational opportunities available to community residents. In addition, a coordinated effort in a community implies that problem-solving efforts will be undertaken by residents representing various walks of life. It also means that educational decisions and many times other kinds of decisions are made by a representative body of individuals and that such information is disseminated throughout the community.

Unfortunately, the coordinating role has not been fulfilled very successfully by adult educators or anyone else in most communities. The horizontal relationships are frequently weak or not established.

There are several exemplary coordination efforts that have been tried or are being tried by adult educators in various communities. Some communities have established a community council of representatives from various adult education agencies which meets regularly for purposes of sharing programming ideas, establishing common calendars, and finding new ways of working together.

The community needs some central place for conducting educational activities. Adult and community educators have been able to establish the community school as such a site in many communities. Some communities have established the YMCA or YWCA, a church, or some other facility as a central gathering spot. A role remaining for adult and community educators is the development of such sites in many additional communities.

The adult educators also should deal with the linking of the home, school, and community. Involving residents in self-determination efforts, designing effective parent education programmes, and keeping a close contact between educators and family members or community leaders are some of the means being employed to meet such a need. No doubt, more can be accomplished, but the growing awareness of education as a lifelong endeavour and the development of such programmes as the community school will continue to strengthen the linking of people and their communities.

Lastly, there is the continuous need for the development of community leadership. Another related need is for individuals willing and capable of undertaking political and civic responsibilities. Consequently, adult educators have a responsibility to train existing leaders and to find ways of continuously developing new community leaders.

The operation of adult education agency programmes, the teaching of adult education classes, and the various human resource development or training jobs are very important to the vitality of almost every community. The successful fulfillment of such roles, all of those described above, and many more just beginning to evolve or not yet even thought of will be crucial as the notion of lifelong learning becomes a societal reality.

11.6.5. Vitalising Educative Class

Most people, organisations, and agencies have a potential and capacity for being a part of the educational process. Thus, in addition to the normal education of youth through a formal school setting, educators in the educative community will need to assume the responsibility of identifying potential resources for education and facilitating their utilisation by people of all ages.

A whole new set of roles for educators and community citizens becomes possible through visualising the multitude of resources as potential teachers or learning means. Teachers learn to supplement education with visits to community sites, parents can supplement their children's education through the use of various community resources; community parks or open areas become sites to study nature or ecology; church leaders provide education to people of all ages in the area of human relationships; and potential community leaders develop their skills of helping others by specific teaching endeavours in a school classroom.

The educated adults in a community will necessitate that educators, parents, and other citizens learn a great deal more about the communities in which they reside. More knowledge about a community and its potential resources for learning can be obtained by personal interviews, mail-out survey forms, the compilation of a directory of existing agencies and their services, and the formation of community task forces whose functions include determining educational resources and helping community residents become aware of such resources.

11.6.6. Activities of Teachers of Adults and Youth

The teachers of adults must possess certain eligibilities. The educational activities of a teacher may need to include occasional visits to homes, the administering of needs-assessment projects, or an involvement with educational programmes outside the school setting. Several of these types of activities will need to become accepted endeavours during the regular working day so school administrators need to be a part of activating the educative community, too.

The growth of community education programmes also necessitate that schools, colleges, universities, and vocational training organisations become familiar with the related philosophy and programming possibilities inherent in the community education movement. Enriching any curriculum with community-related activities and learning is an example of such a philosophy. To help integrate education into the entire life of the community is perhaps one of the most crucial implications for teachers and trainers. This must include identifying potential educational resources and planning for their use, helping interested citizens learn how to use the resources, and adjusting school, higher education, and training curricula to maximise the learning potential of community experiences.

The educators must also help to develop a more extended use of all educational facilities by people of all ages. Keeping public school buildings open more hours each year, utilising existing community athletic and auditorium facilities more extensively, and creating a community center facility are some of the possibilities already being implemented in many communities. Additional uses only need to be experimented with by interested educators and community leaders.

Some of the activities that could be enhanced even more than they are in most colleges and universities are an exposure of students to community theory, the provision of off-campus experiences in community activities, and the development of activating skills. Experienced teachers would no doubt benefit from similar learning opportunities if they are made available through in-service or extension education opportunities.

The collages and universities can also carry out certain roles for spreading adult education. University experts working on special community problems or with special audiences, helping educators at the community level learn how to utilise various nontraditional approaches to education, and carrying out the research necessary to solve various community problems are only some of the possible roles. It is hoped that all educators will accept the challenges presented by a wider use of the community in lifelong learning.

11.7. Conclusion

The successful completion of continuing education and lifelong learning needs total support from the learners, community as well as the state. Each country gives priority to educate its people because the development of a nation depends on the literacy level of its people. The teachers assigned for educating adults must possess certain qualities. So, only with a quantum jump, a nation can espouse success in adult education.

References

Baden, C. (Ed.), *New Directions for Continuing Education: Competitive Strategies for Continuing Education*, No. 35. San Francisco: Jossey-Bass, 1987.

Beder, H. (Ed.), *New Directions for Continuing Education: Marketing Continuing Education*, No. 31. San Francisco: Jossey-Bass, 1986.

Cervero, R.M., and Scanlan, C.L. (Eds.), *New Directions for Continuing Education: Problems and Prospects in Continuing Professional Education*, No. 27. San Francisco: Jossey-Bass, 1985.

Cervero, R., *Effective Continuing Education for Professionals*, San Francisco: Jossey-Bass, 1988.

Candy, P. C., *Self-direction for lifelong learning*, San Francisco: Jossey-Bass, 1991.

Hayes, C. D., *Lifelong learning the search for meaning in a postmodern world*, Wasilla, AK: Autodidactic Press, 1998.

Hesburgh, T. M., Miller, P. A., & Wharton, C. R., *Patterns for lifelong learning*, San Francisco: Jossey-Bass, 1973.

Longworth, N., & Davies, W. K., *Lifelong learning: New vision, new implications, new roles for people, organizations, nations and communities in the 21st century*, Oxford: Kogan Page, 1997.

Merriam, S. B., & Brockett, R. G., *The profession and practice of adult education: An introduction*, San Francisco: Jossey-Bass, 1997.

12

Non-Formal Education and Environmental Protection

12.1. Introduction

The unscrupulous activities of human beings are spoiling our environment and we are in the verge of environmental hazards. Human made wastages is becoming a catastrophe to themselves and nobody seems to stop these deliberate activities. We are breathing polluted oxygen and drinking contaminated water and eating poisonous food products. Every day, many more new types of diseases are emerging and we are unable to find out medicines for some diseases also. These are all the result of our reckless activities which cause irreparable damages in our environment.

People are ignorant about the environment they live in. They are of the opinion that the natural resources are unlimited and they never face a scarcity. Education can made a drastic change in this regard. The environmentalisation of formal and non-formal education brings relevance to teaching/learning at all levels and types of education. Non-formal environmental education with its wide scope and large target audience is a fertile and promising field for fulfilling the purpose of inculcating awareness, knowledge, skills, commitments and actions on the part of individuals and groups in the general public for the protection and improvement of the environment and its quality for the present and future generations.

Non-formal education can do a lot to spread awareness among the people about the environment. But the development of non-formal environmental education requires the incorporation of environmental education objectives, concepts, teaching methods and evaluation techniques into all processes of non-formal education. In order to facilitate the development of non-formal environmental education, it has been considered essential to develop some guidelines to serve as a discussion guide in a series of regional and sub-regional training seminars in which key personnel shall focus on the task of how to environmentalise their non-formal education systems at the national and local levels.

The role of non-formal environmental education is to check man's exploitative attitude towards the environment such as population pressures, rising energy consumption, resource depletion, pollution, ecosystem degradation and urban population explosions. The strength of non-formal education lies in the fact that it does not operate within a given set of rules with a strict structure, curriculum and examination procedures.

Non-formal environmental education, theoretically at least, is more capable of responding to local environmental issues which have more social meaning and usefulness to the community and is less dominated by academic requirements. One of the major problems envisaged concerning the effective implementation of non-formal environmental education is the diversity of the target groups and their needs.

Popular attitudes towards the environment may vary from culture to culture. It is imperative that people foster and develop an environmental ethic which is prudent and conducive to a harmonious development with nature, maintaining stability and sustainability.

12.2. Environmental Education

The living beings all over the world are facing acute shortage of food and drinking water. India has recently experienced the worst environmental accident in living memory and many scientists in the Federal Republic of West Germany believes that they are monitoring the death of the Black Forest by acid deposition. These signs indicate that the magnitude and urgency of solving environmental problems, whether local or global, are not diminishing. While it is difficult, if not impossible, to assess whether world wide, the extent of such problems is increasing or decreasing.

We are approaching very fastly towards disaster and total destruction is its end. The concept of the globe marching slowly towards perfection is untenable, the more cynical might. A more accurate metaphor would portray the world running quickly in the opposite direction. But the way ahead has been signposted for many years.

The world population must be aware of and concerned about, the environment and its associated problems, and which has the knowledge, skills, attitudes, motivations and commitment to work individually and collectively toward solutions of current problems and the prevention of new ones.

The objectives of environmental education are:

— *Awareness*: To help individuals and social groups acquire an awareness of and sensitivity to the total environment and its allied problems.
— *Knowledge*: To help individuals and social groups acquire a basic understanding of the total environment, its associated problems and humanity's critically responsible presence and role in it.
— *Attitude*: To help individuals and social groups acquire social values, strong feelings of concern for the environment and the motivation for actively participating in its Protection and improvement.
— *Skills*: To help individuals and social groups acquire the skills for solving environmental problems.
— *Evaluation ability*: To help individuals and social groups evaluate environmental measures and education programmes in terms of ecological, political, economic, social, aesthetic and educational factors.
— *Participation*: To help individuals and social groups develop a sense of responsibility and urgency regarding environmental problems so as to ensure appropriate action to solve these problems.

Education is a potent force for bringing about change and development and thus environmental education was of paramount importance in developing an environmental ethic based on ecological balance, man's quality of life and the needs of future generations. There is a growing momentum accompanied by the kind of healthy excitement and controversy that occurs with any such reformation.

12.2.1. Trends in Environmental Education

Nobody can live in this earth without natural resources. When we pollute our environment purposefully, we are destroying our life saving devices. So, all human beings must be aware about the intensity of such activities. Education is the only means to make the people aware about the need for protecting our environment. The fundamental aims of environmental education for differing groups within society such as teachers, adults and out-of-school youth, were identified. In addition, the relevance and efficiency of teaching programmes dealing with environmental issues depend on their being specifically adapted to the differing socio-economic conditions within each country.

We must formalise an environmental ethic for the protection of our environment and must solve the problems and learn new ways to come out of this labyrinth. The successful management of the environment depends upon the co-operation of various governmental agencies, industry and concerned, informed citizens acting either individually or through elected officials. The latter group is the most important influence on the environment, the problems of producing an informed citizenry must not be underrated. Intelligent and effective citizen participation in environmental conservation requires knowledge from the sciences, social sciences and humanities. It further requires the development of practical skills which assist people to live in a manner which enhances environmental quality and reduced environmental degradation.

The most significant problem in environmental education today is how to translate, in simple terms, such concepts as interdependence, limitation of finite resources, human population growth and energy flow. In addition the economic advantages of carrying out simple measures associated with the conservation of renewable resources, the planning of land use and the prevention of pollution must also be highlighted. These are not easy tasks. Firstly we must critically examine existing educational practice; we often disregard the extent to which formal education may be a cause of our problems.

Many educators today can be accused of using classical elitist approaches which are old fashioned and irrelevant to the vast majority of school children. Many children throughout the world should be receiving an education which uses the richness of the environment to develop a wide range of cognitive skills rather than focusing on disciplines and Specialisation for selection purposes.

Teachers have an important role in education the new generation about necessity for protecting the environmental. They adopt new techniques in their classroom teaching. Thus an environmental studies approach to teaching should involve the children in such things as working outside the classroom; enquiring, exploring, comparing, contrasting and making decisions and value judgements. It should be based on scientific enquiry while not ignoring the emotional response that can come from the child being closely involved with the biotic features of his environment. But for many teachers, adopting the above approach would entail a complete rejection of existing practice and philosophy; they have not been trained to think or act in this manner.

The environmental problem cannot be solved completely through traditional approach to education. The complexity of most environmental issues mean that they do not fit within the boundaries of any one discipline but are trans disciplinary in nature. Teachers are expected to deal with a situation which is radically different from their own experience and training.

The response of the formal education sector to the environmental challenge worldwide has been slow and piecemeal. It has to be accepted that the educational system, like the rest of society, has not been able to adapt quickly enough to rapidly changing environmental conditions. This situation is unlikely to change dramatically in the next decade and the world cannot wait for a new generation of politicians and decision-makers to emerge.

The development of an educational strategy is prepared to challenge existing economic principles and practice, which questions traditional social and political goals and also critically examines the personal ethics that are considered the norms of many societies. To achieve this in target groups other than pre-primary, primary, secondary and tertiary level students, it is necessary to develop an effective nonformula environmental education process.

Environmental education must be envisaged as a lifelong process and consequently nonformula education is of the utmost importance in creating a society whose citizens are knowledgeable enough to make a valid contribution to the decision making process. All countries in the world should consider how they can extend the educational opportunities for all members of their society; people must learn that the environment determines and shapes their life styles, their expectations and future hopes. Such an insight can only lead to a more concerned and accountable populace for one becomes responsible for what one knows.

12.3. Environmental Problems

Human's lust for amassing money destruct the environment and we are creating irreparable harms on our environment knowingly and unknowingly. On global scale projections concerning the environment, population growth and levels of pollution are pessimistic. There is no change in public policies, institutions or rates of technological change. The major issues and problems confronting man include population, energy, resource depletion, pollution, deforestation, desertification, extinction of species and ecosystem degradation.

12.3.1. Population

The world is on the verge of population explosion and the population is doubling every 20-25 years. Over population leads to hungry, poverty and unemployment. About one third or one half of those alone are hungry or malnourished; three quarters of them do not have either adequate housing or safe water supply. The great majority of human beings in the world today have to live on $100 per year and many spend most of their waking hours and 60-95% of their incomes just trying to get enough food for themselves and their children to prevent starvation or debilitating diseases. No completely technological solution to this complex problem exists.

The problem is aggravating because the food production is not increasing in proportion to the increase in population. The cultivable land is shrinking day by day. People are converting the fertile land for constructing buildings. The food supplies can increase only by putting more land under cultivating freshwater and oceans and raising yields by using new seeds, increased irrigation, use of fertiliser etc. However, it is necessary to develop integrated plans for reducing world population birth rates, controlling agricultural pollution and mounting a massive attack on global poverty.

12.3.2. Energy

With the development of nation, the people consume more energy. The demand for energy is doubling every 14 years, and most of the energy is consumed by industrial nations; while they only have 30% of the world's population, but they use 80% of the world energy. Many forms of agriculture today are dependent upon substantial energy subsidies i.e. the addition of fossil fuel energy to supplement the input of energy through photosynthesis to agricultural systems.

Huge energy consumption leads to pollution and it will ultimately create environmental problems. Concentrations of carbon dioxide in the atmosphere have ensued and may possibly lead to a warming of the earth's climate. Increased levels of sulphur and nitrogen oxides lead to the formation of acid rain and the loss of trees and animals in forests and lakes. An increasing level of radiation in the environment due to accidents associated with nuclear power; nuclear fission is potentially the most hazardous of all sources of energy. Alternative non-polluting energy sources such as hydroelectric, wind, tidal power, geothermal solar energy etc must be explored for other use.

Unless people make use of alternative energy sources like bio-energy, the whole living beings should have paid the brunt of attack. Bio energy can play an important role in providing for future energy needs. Biomass (plant material) is a widely available resource that can be produced renewably and in many situations at low costs. Not only does it reduce dependence on costly oil imports, but its low sulphur, low ash and high oxygen content makes biomass clean and easy to convert to high quality synthetic fuels.

The development of Biogas in India and China has met with varying degrees of success. China in particular is very committed to continued promotion of Biogas and it has been declared a principal alternative to cope with the fuel crisis of rural Chinese villages, however there is some apprehension concerning the future of Biogas, due to the threat of modernisation. Many developing countries are forced to pay a large proportion of their foreign exchange earnings to secure oil, hence slowing down development. A large proportion of the oil is used in transport. One feasible substitute for oil is ethanol which is made from carbohydrate producing crops.

12.3.3. Resource Depletion

There are two types of resources available on earth, renewable and non-renewable. Renewable resources are those which can maintain themselves and can be replenished by crops, forests, wildlife, air water and soil. Other resources such as oil, natural gas, coals, phosphates and metal ores are non-renewable. However, the usefulness of certain resources changes with our technological progress e.g. increases in synthetics vs. non-synthetics such as rubber. A substance becomes or remains a resource because technology makes it available for a reasonable cost.

12.3.4. Pollution

The most lethal problem earth faces is pollution. It occurs when excessive amounts of waste accumulate in the environment and affect humans and plants or animals in an undesirable way, usually by causing environmental stress. Pollutants can range from those producing high environmental stress such as heavy metals, solider radio active wastes to those raising a lower level of stress such as litter, noise and low levels of carbon monoxide. It is very important to understand how a pollutant behaves within the environment, especially at what concentration it is stressful. The level or threshold at which a pollutant can harm varies widely between pollutant and with different organisms. Pollutants may combine and have a more severe effect than the sum of the two acting separately.

Pollutants such as DDT and heavy metals (e.g. Mercury) may be concentrated in food chains (biological magnification). It can be appreciated that problems of pollution may be global (e.g. carbon dioxide build-up in the atmosphere) and warrant intergovernmental regulation, national (e.g. toxic waste) or local or regional (river pollution, land fill).

12.3.5. Deforestation

In the name of development and for satisfying the thirst for making money, people are competitively cutting down the life saving device, trees. One of the most rapidly vanishing living natural resources the tropical rain forest is disappearing at a rate of 7.3 million hectares a year. Half the world's plants and animal genetic diversity is concentrated on only 60% of the land surface, mostly in the tropical rain forests.

If unchecked, mankind may witness the elimination of one million of the planet's S-10 million plant and animal species by the end of the century. Through their genetic resources, these species provide essential materials for agriculture, medicine and industry and other economic uses. Most of the loss is occurring in the humid forests of Africa, Asia and South America. Deforestation and mismanagement of the land (e.g. poor soil conservation and badly planned irrigation schemes) have a very significant effect on water availability.

12.3.6. Urban Explosion

The over populated cities is another major problem. For getting employment and a living, people are flooding to towns and cities. This creates imbalances and a lot of environmental problems. From 1900 to 1975 the number of inhabitants in cities with populations over one million has increased tenfold and that of cities with over five million inhabitants multiplied by twenty. During the same time, the population of the twenty five largest cities is more than quadrupled and increased eight to ten times by the year 2000, increasing their average size from two to sixteen million inhabitants.

In the metropolitan areas of the developed countries with low growth or falling pollutions, the problem today is one of reviving activity, preserving the cultural heritage, preventing the depreciation of certain districts before they are transformed into ghettos and making the best possible use of existing infrastructures. The metropolitan areas of developing countries, on the other hand are seeking to control their demographic growth, to organise urban extensions, to make good their lack of facilities and services and make productive use of the available labour force.

The cities and towns are cultivating greeneries in order to reduce some of the social and environmental problems. These green belts help to halt blanket urbanisation; urban renewal is an essential factor in improved integration of inhabitants; planning must be smaller in scale and better adapted for the urban environment and implemented after community participation; energy conservation techniques must be developed. All these developments have to be appropriate to local technical, administrative and financial contexts.

Environmental problems are differ in their extent, diversity and complexity. Procedures for implementing changes vary from country to country and location to location; hence it is essential that participation of citizens in environmental issues and planning procedures is advocated in order to produce the best chance of success for the projects.

12.3.7. Resolving Environmental Problems

12.3.7.1. Community participation

The environmental problems have developed as life threatening hazards. A collective support is needed for checking these problems. It can be either defensive mitigating against change or developmental in which the participants attempt to alter the situation. The type of participation depends upon the nature of the problem and it is often a mixture of both defensive and developmental participation. One aim of participation would be to broaden the base of participants, for instance increasing the social activity of women or illiterates. Groups may be clearly recognised and have a firm structure or less clearly recognised and incidental (e.g. local community action groups). Much depends upon the permanence of the problem.

The communities can also do a lot of things for preserving the nature. In community participation projects, decisions are made in the best interest of the groups and not individuals; however much depends upon the political framework, in some countries defensive groups are treated with deep suspicion and intolerance. In countries operating a democratic parliamentary system, many environmental protest groups have made an impact on the power structure by directly lobbying members of parliament, in some cases, due to insensivity of governments the same groups have concentrated on more direct action or publicised their protests by attracting extensive media coverage (e.g. Greenpeace).

The community participation is an inseparable part of development in developing countries. Participation in implementing projects reduces their cost by mobilising unused local resources and free human energy. Participation in decision-making provides planners with much better information on peoples' wants and dislikes. It helps to avoid disastrous errors which may result if the supposed beneficiaries are not consulted. It can boost morale, increase productivity and reduce negative and destructive conflicts between managers and the managed. In many cases, the poor live in a state of passive inertia because of their total powerlessness in the face of entrenched elites.

The participation is an educative process. It produces confidence in the participants especially in their ability to control circumstances instead of being controlled by them. It can also increase political stability by reducing sectional interest Increased participation will mean a considerable measure of self help but the necessary technical skills, materials and finance have to be provided so assisted self help is required.

12.3.7.2. Spread of awareness

People must be aware of the grave consequences of their activities. There are several stages in the development of environmental awareness, participation and action. The sitting of a factory resulted in an air pollution which caused the local community to be exposed to smoke, steam, dirt and most controversially incompletely burnt toxins. This was initially perceived by the local residents as a nuisance, they then formed a small community protest group which discussed the problem collected and clarified information. They published their activities by holding meetings in schools and developed a publicity drive, which involved contact with local radio, television, producing posters and organising demonstrations.

12.3.7.3. Alternative technologies

Technologies are inevitable for the development of a nation. But the technologies must be environment friendly. The development of alternative technologies (AT) or soft technologies are characterised by ecological self sufficiency, smallness and suited to the economic conditions in developing countries.

The aim of alternative technology is to make the most economical use of a country's natural resources and its capital, labour and skills that further national and social goals; the objective is to foster the right choice of technology. In developing countries, the appropriate technology should create as many jobs as possible-and enable and improve income. It must use scarce capital wisely, using simple machinery and produce goods suited to the local market. Environmentally, the technology should be hygienic, conservational and non polluting; using renewable sources of energy and raw materials with the maximum re-use of industrial and human wastes, and farm residues.

People have basic needs. The alternative technology should satisfy these basic needs and involve popular participation. It must be technically sound, economic to users and customers in comparison with the alternatives and be socially acceptable in the light of local cultures and traditions. The auto rickshaw is an ingenious adaptation of a clever piece of western technology adapted to an eastern need. Solar energy has a big future in the tropics. Alternatives to large conventional energy plants, which are of little use to the poor who cannot afford domestic connections are solar energy and planting of fast growing fuel wood plantations such as eucalyptus. Another appropriate fuel with considerable potential is methane gas from the fermentation of animal and human waste. Unfortunately research into appropriate technology is minimal while that in developing new technology is far greater.

12.3.7.4. *Need for cultivating values in school level*

Nobody can live in this world by destroying the nature. The life of all living beings depends on nature. A little variation on environment also creates huge impacts on the life of all. So, the new generation should bring up by understanding the importance of nature and the consequence if it is destroyed. The concern with out-of-school or non-formal education is likely to promote a deeper understanding of the environment as a living, integrated and interactive system.

12.3.7.5. Conserving environment

The body of every living being is made up of substances from earth. There will not be an iota of life after the destruction of environment. One outcome anticipated from combining intellectual endeavour with manual work is to lay the basis for a more rational approach to the use of the environment in general and the mode of development of its resources in particular. This would help to conserve and find the best use for resources or establish the best means to exploit them, whilst at the same time minimising negative environmental impacts.

12.3.7.6. Rural and urban environments

People are largely migrating to cities and towns in search of job and better living conditions. But this creates ecological imbalances. Improving social and economic conditions in the countryside, by making them more attractive places in which to live and work, would help to reduce flows of migrants from the relatively impoverished rural areas to the more attractive and richer cities but which already have over-burdened social and economic infrastructural facilities.

Resolving infrastructural imbalances between town and country would in the long term relieve some of the pressure of migration from cities and would improve the economic viability of rural economies by reducing rates of abandonment of small properties, at the same time providing better access for small farmers to facilities such as credit and rural extension. In this way they would be better able to sustain their small-scale agricultural economies whilst at the same time making a more significant contribution to the larger national economy.

Through time, both rural and urban environments would become more productive than otherwise : urban places, because their economies would have to support fewer 'dependent' urban migrants; and rural places, because by retaining more people in the countryside with better supporting service back-up a more rational and more extended pattern of agricultural land use could be anticipated.

12.3.7.7. Community and environment

The industrial development in urban creates ecological

imbalances. This characteristic of modern western nations has given rise to conflictual rather than harmonious social and economic relations; these, are manifest for example in the antagonistic dichotomies between urban and rural places and between industry and agriculture. In contrast, the non-formal education and development processes in Cuba, China and Tanzania have been concerned to establish more even, rurally oriented development patterns. Not only is this intended to focus development in the Third World upon those who are most often overlooked but does so in ways which encourage rural people themselves to participate in the process rather than to be merely spectators of it.

People must be aware of the importance of keeping ecological balance. The non-formal educational means by which this is achieved ought not to be underemphasised namely principles such as combining intellectual with manual work, bringing together students and rural workers and training students as producers first and as consumers second. In combination the nature of the development processes and the means by which they have been carried through have avoided creating the geographical dichotomies of developed and undeveloped places and, amongst the population, the antagonisms which have attended modernisation in the west.

12.4. Non-formal Environmental Education

Unpolluted and undistorted environment is our priceless asset. Every individual has the responsibility to preserve it. People make harm on environment due to ignorance. So, we must be properly educated to protect it. We must be aware about the negative impact of our activities. The planning, organisation and methodology of non-formal environmental education varies enormously from one country to another. In Nepal, for example, Radio Nepal broadcasts a regular weekly programme on ecology with an emphasis on the preservation of forests, a particular problem in Nepal. The Iraqui Environmental Protection Society has confined its activities to the production of publications aimed at stimulating public awareness. The Nature Protection League of Poland, in co-operation with various youth and adult groups, has set up school nature camps and environmental research centres for young naturalist.

Many regional nature museums and gardens have special educational rooms for environmental education In Indonesia, the Government accepted that a non-formal environmental education programme was needed to enhance public awareness of environmental problems. Consequently a team of non-formal educators based its campaign on local environmental issues. The public is reached through a regular series of lectures to youth and women's organisations and these are augmented by an input from the mass media - radio, T.V. and the press where the particular target group is children outside the formal education system.

It is the duty of the authorities to educate on environment to those who are kept out of formal education. The type of non-formal environmental education may be classified as either participatory or non-participatory. The latter are those in which target group members are merely passive receivers and would include radio and T.V. broadcasts, press articles, visits to institutions such as museums, zoos, aquaria etc., and also listening to the occasional lecture at a local club. These non-participatory forms of non-formal environmental education are very prevalent throughout the world, particularly so in the developed countries.

People can be educated by using the entertainment mediums like Radio, TV, etc. During the last decade, the increased incidence of T.V. programmes dealing with environmental problems such as conservation, pollution, famine etc, is a measure of the concern felt by the general public for these important issues. It is difficult to assess the value and effectiveness of the learning situation in these non-participatory activities because little research has been undertaken.

The TV programmes have a greater influence on people. But the impact of T.V. programmes on the development of an environmental ethic has not been studied but it would appear that such programmes have been instrumental in creating a groundswell of public opinion that has manifested itself in such NO's as Greenpeace and Friends of the Earth. The goal of these, and similar organisations throughout the world, is to sensitise the general public to environmental issues, to raise the level of environmental awareness and understanding and also to encourage active participation in environmental problem solving. In West Germany the "Greens" have been able to give a political dimension to this environmental concern and were able to win a number of seats in the elected parliament.

12.4.1. Non-Participatory Programmes

The main concern of non-participatory programmes is to entertain the viewers, they are also instrument in bringing about attitudinal changes in a large number of the world's population. It is interesting to record that in a regional conference on "Environmental Education in ASEAN Universities and its Transfer" held in the University.

Disadvantages of formal education system are lack of resources, high drop-out rates and insufficient placements at secondary school and subsequently the non-formal environmental education programmes of a participatory nature assume an increased significance. Each region of the world offers numerous examples of such programmes and it would be salutary to examine some of the more common methods of instruction used in non-formal environmental education with particular reference to the various target groups. The talk or lecture as part of an extended programme. This type of teaching involves one person talking to an audience on a particular subject.

The technique requires little active participation by the audience and is, therefore, probably the least significant in helping the learning process. It is also the teaching technique which most closely mirrors that used in formal education; it highlights the distinction between teacher and taught and this could be disadvantageous if the audience has a high percentage of individuals who have not experienced success in the formal sector e.g. school drop outs and early school leavers. Paradoxically, it may be a good technique for a class of adults who are experiencing a traditional classroom situation for the first time. Whatever the audience however, there are certain features of the technique which should be borne in mind by all educators.

The classroom should be adequately ventilated, well lighted and be at a reasonable temperature. Students should be comfortable but not pampered. The seating arrangement will depend upon the size of the class but it should be such that all the class can see the face of the speaker.

The technical competence of the speaker the speaker must be aware of those features of the talk that encourage the audience to continue listening and avoid those which do the opposite i.e. send them to sleep. The most common fault is that the speaker talks too quickly. This is often because too much is being attempted; most non-formal classes can only cope with a small number of ideas at any one time. Adult audiences in particular, need time to consider and understand what they are hearing and often the same point or idea needs to be repeated in a variety of ways.

The speaker reads from a prepared text in a boring monotone. The soporific effect of such a delivery can be counteracted by the speaker consciously introducing variation in volume and pitch and also pausing at significant places during the lecture. In general it must be appreciated that the span of attention for most classes in non-formal environmental education is very limited, probably some ten to fifteen minutes. After this period of time, involuntary breaks in attention become increasingly common when little of what is heard is comprehended. The speaker must not confuse interest with understanding.

Many of the environmental issues which need to be considered by non-formal classes are very relevant and of immediate concern to the audience and thus motivation may be high. But such issues may also be very complicated and the process of identifying and understanding an environmental problem and exploring alternative strategies of solving it, may be a long, slow and often frustrating experience. The speaker, therefore, when planning a talk should ensure that not too much is attempted with the significant points being made early in the talk. Frequent recapitulations should be made in a variety of ways and the end of the talk should contain an effective and stimulating summary.

12.4.2. Classroom Discussion

Discussions always help to acquire knowledge. It widens the thinking capacity and helps to go for deep in a problem. This form of teaching is obviously more participatory than the talk or lecture and is, therefore, potentially a more effective teaching and learning strategy. It is also a technique which is particularly suitable for non-formal environmental education because many adults can learn best in a social context. Participation in a group discussion can often boost the confidence of students, an important factor in self development. It would be irresponsible, however, to suggest that discussion as a teaching technique has no drawbacks.

A discussion session in a non-formal class provides the opportunity for people to express firmly held prejudices or irrational arguments and little, if any, dialogue occurs. Similarly the discussion may be monopolised by a few vociferous class members may accentuate or produce a feeling of inferiority in other members of the class. It is most important that the teacher or group leader, in particular, does not assume a dominant role in discussion sessions, a tendency all too apparent in many non-formal classes.

But discussion, as a teaching strategy, is not appropriate where practical skills are being acquired such as the use of unknown agricultural implements e.g. crop hand sprayers or the application and use of simple environmental monitoring equipment. Under these circumstances, clear, unambiguous instructions need to be understood by the class and a discussion on the relative merits of one machine versus another may be counterproductive.

If the number of students in a classroom is large, discussion is inappropriate. It would appear that good discussion practice becomes very difficult when class numbers exceed twenty five with an optimum number between ten and fifteen. Probably the greatest difficulty with this teaching technique is the fact that, on many occasions, either the members of the class have nothing to contribute or they are incapable of adequately expressing themselves in a group situation. In such circumstances the discussion session must be seen as part of a total teaching strategy.

12.4.3. Cracking Problems

Nobody can hide from problems. In other words, life itself is a problem. Education helps to face the problems in life. Environmental education has been considered essentially as education for discovery and action. This implies a teaching methodology that gives equal importance to the analytical and theoretical-approach of the scientific method as well as to the more synthetic and pragmatic problem-solving approach. This technique is not difficult to understand for problem solving not only provides a basis for a relevant and meaningful curriculum, it is also highly participatory and allows individuals to develop critical thinking skills which are transferable to many other situations. Furthermore success in a problem-solving situation, no matter how small and insignificant, can lead to a much improved self image.

People can become change agents for the benefit of themselves and their society. But the persistence of many environmental problems indicates that there are a limited number of people who are trained to identify and effectively solve complex environmental problems. It also indicates that problem solving is a difficult process and, furthermore, using problem solving as a teaching technique equally arduous. Some of the latter difficulties arise from constraints within existing formal systems and may be overcome by developing problem solving programmes in the non-formal system.

According to the target group and with the size and complexity of the problem, the methodology associated with environmental problem solving will vary. There are guidelines, however, which should be standard practice in all situations.

12.4.4. Role of the Teacher

Teachers should be the carriers of light which leads to life not towards destruction. They should be the embodiment of values. They are the people who bear the wand to carve the future of a nation. Most learning is not the result of instruction. It is rather the result of unhampered participation in a meaningful setting. The teacher's role is to guide, clarify, co-ordinate, encourage and if possible, determine the boundaries of the problem study. The latter is important because the group should experience same degree of success in its project.

The teachers should inculcate values in the minds of students. The selection of the particular environmental problem to be examined should come from discussions within the target study group. The teacher or group leader may wish to suggest alternative problems to be considered, ensuring that such alternatives are of a practical, pragmatic nature and capable of being solved, but in the final analysis high levels of motivation can only be maintained if the group determines the problems to be investigated.

We can solve environmental problems only through education. The teacher/group leader should ensure that the maximum use is made of the knowledge, expertise and experience possessed by members of the group. The problem to be examined will be of a local nature and this will require local knowledge and local experience. The teacher should ensure that contributions from the local officials of various government agencies, e.g. health, water, agricultural extension officer, wildlife ranger etc, are received and understood by the target group but the fund of relevant information collectively possessed by group members should never be underestimated.

Environmental education must adopt a problem solving approach, which can make individuals aware of those features in their environment which are detrimental to individual and collective well-being. It can also teach them how to analyse the causes of problems and take appropriate counter measures. By working together communities do have the ability to plan for sustainable development within the context of living resource conservation.

12.4.5. Awareness Making through Arts

Arts have a wider influence on individual. The use of drama/popular theatre as a communication medium for development projects has a long history. In the late 40's, teams of field-workers toured villages in Ghana using drama and demonstration to educate and involve people in campaigns for such topics as family planning, child care, cocoa disease eradication etc.

The programmes were mainly designed to impart information and skills. They were planned and prepared by headquarters staff of various government departments such as agriculture, and health and little, if any, consultation occurred with the rural clientele.

12.4.6. Spreading Awareness in a Vast Area

The earth is on the path of destruction because of the wrong doings of the people. Knowingly or unknowingly, people are destroying the environment. People should be aware about the impact of their activities. Environmental education and existing non-formal education programmes many of the techniques are currently practised by some programmes of non-formal education. The scale and range of existing programmes in the non-formal sector of education are enormous and offer a great opportunity for the spread of environmental education. Many countries throughout the world are attempting to deal with the problem of illiteracy by mounting adult, functional literacy projects. Such projects are fertile ground for introducing those environmental issues which are of immediate concern and relevance to the participants. This must go beyond the obvious teaching ploy of ensuring that readers, flashcards, booklets etc, deal with everyday features of adult life and work.

Through education, we can preserve our nature. The acquisition of adult literacy is enhanced by the participants considering environmental problems that affect the lives of themselves and their families. Thus an examination of how to improve the amenities of a village such as a constant water supply and adequate sanitation arrangements, or how to improve the economy of an area by increased agricultural yields and better marketing, would appear to be ideal topics for an adult literacy class.

An environmental perspective is not perceived as an esoteric, abstract notion, counterproductive in some way to local developmental strategies. It rust be explained, simply and clearly, how environmental objectives can contribute, both in the long- and short-term to such development programmes. Once again this presupposes that the teachers or extension workers engaged in such programmes have a background in environmental education which enables them to give this broader view. In order that this is achieved, a more radical approach to the training of adult education personnel is needed. Instead of being trained to teach courses which may be narrowly conceived e.g. use of fertilisers, prevention of specific diseases, pre- and ante-natal care; all adult education tutors should be trained in the broader perspective of environmental education.

12.5. Training Programmes for Teachers

Teachers have a bigger responsibility in spreading environmental education. They must take this responsibility responsibly and should educate students the need for preserving environment. In order to devise effective training programmes for potential teachers of environmental education in the non-formal sector, it is essential to identify the needs and requirements of the different target groups and thus plan the appropriate training programmes. Any schedule for training personnel involved in non-formal education should include items which are of significance to the particular target group.

12.5.1. Ecological Basis

Teachers should be able to apply a knowledge of ecological foundations to predict the ecological consequences of alternative solutions to environmental problems; be sufficiently literate in ecology to identify, select and interpret appropriate sources of scientific information in a continuing effort to investigate, evaluate and find solutions for environmental problems; communicate and apply in an educational context, the major concepts in ecology.

12.5.2. Conceptual Awareness

Teachers are the role models for students and they learn and try to follow the opinions of teachers. So, the teachers should not be degraded as machines. Instead, they should be able to select, develop and/or implement curricular materials which will effectively make receivers aware of how man's cultural activities (e.g. religious, economic, political, social, etc) influence the environment from an ecological perspective.

The teachers must also analyse the impact on the environment from an ecological perspective; a wide variety of local, regional, national and international environmental issues and the ecological and cultural implications of these issues. They must be also aware about the viable alternative solutions available for remediating discrete environmental issues and the ecological and cultural implications of these alternative solutions; the need for environmental issue investigation and evaluation as a pre-requisite to sound decision making the roles played by differing human values in environmental issues and the need for personal value clarification as an integral part of environmental decision making the need for responsible citizenship action (e.g. persuasion, consumerism, legal action, political action, eco-management) in the remediation of environmental issues.

12.5.3. Skills

The minimum requirement of a teacher, who undertakes environmental issues, is he/she should be competent to take positive environmental action for the purpose of achieving and/ or maintaining a dynamic equilibrium between quality of life and the quality of environment, and to develop, select and/or implement curricular materials and strategies to develop similar competencies in receivers to take individual or group action when appropriate (i.e. persuasion, consumerism, political action, legal action, eco-management, or combinations of these action categories).

The teachers should have a sound knowledge of ecological principles and conservation practices but of equal importance is the need for teachers to be sympathetic to the aims and objectives of non-formal environmental education. Thus they must have experience in their training which helps them to develop a sensitivity to the needs of the target group and to the individuals who compose it.

The teachers must learn to identify with, and be sympathetic to, the difficulties and problems faced by members of their class. In establishing relationships with, class members they must learn to recognise the virtues inherent in every human being. Pride is the besetting sin of teachers and they must understand that the flaunting of a superior intellect is counter productive to the aims of non-formal environmental education. Because of the complexity of many issues in E-E., most, if not all teachers, will find themselves in situations that are beyond their own expertise and experience.

The teachers must also be prepared to admit their ignorance and this can be difficult if the teacher has adopted a highly autocratic posture with the students. Humility, integrity and sincerity are the behavioural characteristics that underpin the best human relationships; such relationships based on a mutual trust and confidence is the keystones of learning in non-formal education.

12.5.4. Role of Radio

Radio has a wider audience even in the era of information technology. The use of radio in developing an awareness of the environment and environmental issues has been a characteristic of the medium since its origin. However, most programme producers, outside the traditional formal school framework are often more concerned with education by stealth rather than signposting programmes as environmental education.

Portable, transistorised radio has become the most widespread and commonly used invention of the twentieth century. Thus radio has been, and is likely to be for some time, the main medium for non-formal education in the developing world. One of the major problems of using radio for educational purposes is that of ensuring that the message reaches, and is understood by the target audience and many strategies have been tried to increase feedback from listeners.

The impact of radio programmes has been minimal in nearly all of the countries where this strategy has been attempted. The reasons for this are numerous and include lack of finance, an absence of a support infrastructure and, perhaps, an overemphasis on literacy and basic education. Another factor affecting the widespread success of the radio learning group strategies is the lack of message specificity. People, both in rural and urban areas are motivated by issues that have significance to their day-to-day lives.

People's etiquette is the best solution for solving environmental problems. Many environmental problems are localised, or have a local manifestation, and need to be discussed and, hopefully, solved by local people and local officials. It is often not appropriate to confront people with problems that are at a worldwide or even national level; they need to examine the problems of their village or their town such as their water supply, the use of fertilisers on their fields, the graffiti in their town centre etc.

12.5.5. Television

The idiot's box has dominated the minds of all with information and entertainment. Television has enormous potential to inform, fascinate, stimulate and challenge people's views on environmental issues but, even more so than radio, it lacks a local perspective. The costs of producing television programmes and the concern of the producers with viewing ratings means that it is unlikely that coverage of small-scale, local environmental issues will occur and even major environmental problems which are not newsworthy will be ignored. Thus television, as with radio, has to be localised and people who traditionally are the "object audience" have to become "subject participants in the message.

Video can provide the answer in that it can be the means whereby television is used in a locally-based participating style of non-formal environmental education. In the developed world, video has become a major tool at all levels of formal education but its use in non-formal education is not widespread. In the developing world, although it is use was at first spasmodic and ill-defined, it is now being used more extensively to train extension workers of various government departments.

The impact of television and radio programmes can be consolidated and extended by the use of suitable written materials. Thus associated teaching aids such as posters, flip-charts, field guides, instruction manuals etc; are of great importance in all forms of non-formal education. Such a multi-media approach has been shown to be most effective in disseminating knowledge, attitudes and skills to the general public.

12.6. Ethics in Environmental Education

People should follow some environment ethics in their life to lead a peaceful and healthy life. Our life is tied up with nature, and without nature, nobody can exist in this world. Environmental attitudes and ethics vary from culture to culture and are influenced by societal, theological and environmental factors. An environmental ethic is composed of three main elements:

i) Harm to people

ii) Harm to plants and animals

iii) Harm to natural systems

In India, all religious scriptures reiterate the importance of nature and these Holy books portrait the life of humans which go together with nature. An environmental ethic has been present from the original speciation of man, and is inherent in all religious beliefs. A chief observance of Buddhists is the role of sanctity of all life forms. The various Indian tribes had a deep respect for the environment, indeed they recognised that the earth had a spirit. When Black Elk, a holy man of the Oglala Sioux, speaks of "the beauty and strangeness of the earth" he speaks of reverence for the everyday environment, an environment which was interwoven with Indian life. The closeness to which the Indians felt attached to the earth is mirrored in Indian sayings and statements from their people.

In primitive age, people literally love soil and they sat or reclined on the ground with a feeling of being close to a mothering fewer. It was good for the skin to touch the earth and the old people liked to remove their moccasins and walk with bare feet on the sacred earth. Their tipis were built on the earth and their altars made of earth. The birds that flew in the air came to rest upon the earth and it was the final abiding place of all things that lived and grew.

With industrialisation, people are going away and away from the nature. Today, nobody like to lead a life by moving with nature. Man's heart away from nature becomes hard and that a lack of respect for growing, living things soon led to the lack of respect for humans as well. While this deeply spiritual environmental ethic may exist in many cultures in less developed countries, it has declined in the western world. Despite this many are aware of the loss, particularly the dehumanising and desocialising effects of rapid industrialisation and urbanisation and its effect on the environment.

The development of an environmental philosophy evaluates the relationship between man and his fellow beings and their relationship to the biophysical surroundings. Environmental philosophy provides an important contemplative perspective to a mode of thinking that is concerned with the application of management techniques and political activism motivated to sustain. Often the formulation and development of an environmental philosophy involves the resolution of contradictory elements which are considered e.g. the environmental curtailment of freedom, protection of sovereignty and questions of moral and cultural rights.

Environmental philosophy aims to develop an ethic which facilitates a prudent attitude and practice towards the environment. A variety of different views are held within the western world. The eco-centric attitude is one which has little faith in large scale technology, believes materialism for its own sake is wrong and in the intrinsic importance of nature for the humanity of man and has a high regard for the idea that ecological laws dictate human morality. The technocentric attitude has a strong faith that man will find a way out of difficulties either politically or technologically.

The self reliant soft technologist has much to offer developing countries whose people have the will to develop independently. The soft technologists have little faith in large scale technology and its associated demands on elitist expertise, central state authority and inherently anti democratic institutions. They emphasise smallness of scale and hence community identity in settlement work and leisure, the integration of concepts of work and leisure through a process of personal involvement and communal improvement. They place importance upon participation in community, affairs and guarantees of the rights of minority interests.

To maintain the sustainability of finite ecosystems is one of the most pressing environmental problems. Many believe a solution to this problem lies in a harmonious collaboration with nature and control based upon ecological understanding and the ethic of stewardship. In order to transform a destructive attitude towards the environment to one resulting in a sustainable earth it may be necessary to develop a number of approaches, ecological, humanistic and theological.

Today, people are going against the nature. The man vs. nature attitude of each culture arose historically, but more challenging and vital, cultures may attempt to develop environmentally aware attitudes and to seek alternatives. These must evolve towards forming a partnership with nature based upon ecological understanding and co-operation; with an emphasis on preserving and encouraging physical, biological and cultural diversity, while preventing the deterioration of the quality of the environment. The ideal human goal is that of caring and sharing, not complete individualism and domination. No individual or group has the right to an ever increasing share of earth's finite resources.

12.7. Managing Non-formal Environmental Education

The environmental problem is a global phenomenon. So, every individual and each and every nation has the responsibility to keep nature pure. A number of international organisations which have been involved in non-formal environmental education include the Food and Agriculture Organisation (F.A.O.), World Health Organisation (WHO) and the Meteorological Organisation (WO). The United Nations Children's Fund (UNICEF), in particular, have emphasised the role of non-formal education in helping people interact with their environment in mutually constructive ways. UNESCO plays a key role both in general environmental education in all its aspects (both formal and non-formal).

The International Environmental Education Programme (I.E.E.P.) has contributed greatly to the development of environmental awareness, particularly by initiating a series of international and regional meetings which led to the governmental Conference at Tbilisi in 1977. The Conference laid the basis for the development of national strategies and the promotion of international co-operation.

Educational goals are defined in different ways by different groups and different processes are thought to be essential for their attainment. One way to partially resolve the problem is to consider the perception of environmental education as a transaction in which everyone should have a role to play. It is necessary to develop a forum for non-formal environmental education where all representatives can interact and consider suggestions for action. A forum can be developed at national levels to allow participation by a greater number from the grass roots of each nation.

Non-formal environmental education at national levels environmental education has an inextricable place within the concept of non-formal education particularly in the developing countries because of its link with basic needs and development, voluntary and governmental organisations tend not to be well co-ordinated, although co-peration between voluntary organisations is growing e.g. council for environmental education in Britain.

12.8. Conclusion

The objectives of non-formal environmental education are similar to those in the formal system, that is, to increase awareness and knowledge and to develop skills and attitudes conducive to a harmonious relationship with the environment. To do this, it is necessary to evaluate both environmental education programmes and the efficacy of decisions involved in environmental management. There are strong arguments that prudent environmental decision-making and educational programmes must involve a higher degree of participation in order to develop a sense of responsibility and urgency within the learners. A variety of environmental problems has been reviewed. All countries have some problems and they may be very severe in many Third World countries. Yet, in almost all cases, there are alternative strategies such as more appropriate technological developments or alternative agricultural practices.

There will be a great variety in the form and practice of non-formal environmental education. If the rapid growth in communications technology, which more areas of the world have experienced in the last decade, continues for the next decade, then it is not difficult to envisage systems of teaching/learning evolving that are fundamentally different from those of today.

References

Bennett, D., "The evaluation of environmental education learning", UNESCO in *Trends in Environmental Education*, 1977.

Cowan, M., Denzer, S., Deutsch, D, Dos Santos, A, Lambeth, E, Norton, C, Shackleford, J, Stapp, W, Vincent, L, Wilson, T, Yandala, D, Zimbelman K., "The handling of controversy and problem solving in environmental education", *Environmental Education and Information*, Vol. 3. No. 4, 1985.

Emellin, L., "Environmental Education programme for Adults", In *Trends in Environmental Education*, UNESCO, 1977.

Final report: Intergovernmental Conference on Environmental Education, Paris, France, 1978.

Moemeka, A.A., "Radio's role in non-formal education", *Prospects vol. 13,* part 4., 1983.

O'riordan, T., *Environmentalism,* Pion Press, 1978.

Oyasi, H., "International and regional co-operation in environmental education", In *Trends in Environmental Education,* UNESCO, 1977.

Pirages, D, and Ehrlich, P., *Arkill : Social response to Environmental Imperatives,* San Francisco W.H. Freeman Press, 1974.

Stapp, WB, Cox, D.A., *Environmental Education Activities Manual,* Thomson-Shore, Dexter, Michigan, U.S.A, UNESCO, 1981.

13

Typology of Alternative Education Programmes

13.1. Introduction

Education has the vital part in everybody's life. But circumstances prevent many to attain this. For such people, alternative education is a blessing. It is the study or practice of implementing alternative schools or programmes. Public alternative education serves to ensure that every young person may find a path to the educational goals of the community. Alternative schools and programmes focus on what they can offer the student, not on what problems the student has had in the past. Alternative education is a vital component of the total educational system.

A poor country like India, education is a wild goose chase for most of the people. In a struggle to meet both ends, they compromise with education and stop learning. They are unable to go for formal education. Alternative education programme is meant for educating those who discontinue their education before completion. It is defined as an instructional programme, approved by the school board, that utilises successful alternative or adaptive school structures and teaching techniques and that is incorporated into existing, traditional classrooms or regularly scheduled curricular programmes or that is offered in place of regularly scheduled curricular programmes. Alternative education does not include a private school or a home-based private educational programme.

All educational activities that fall outside the traditional school system comes under alternative education. Ironically, many of these programmes are associated with unsuccessful students and are thought to be dumping grounds for "problem" youth and yet because they represent a departure from the standard approach to schooling, many alternative education programmes of them are known for their innovation and creativity. High quality alternative education programmes are generally known for their adherence to youth development principles.

If effectively implement, the education helps to address the specific needs of children from various racial and ethnic groups and those with special needs (including students with learning or other disabilities that have not yet been identified). Given their importance in the public education system, states and communities are increasingly turning their attention to alternative education issues.

All people have the right to get good education and so is the vulnerable youth who are disconnected from mainstream schools. They need and deserve to have high-quality alternative education. By including in a typology factors associated with quality and effectiveness, policy makers, practioners, and funders may be better able to help promote the expansion of high-quality approaches and improve or eliminate low-quality approaches.

Many of the very first alternative education programmes defined themselves in opposition to the existing educational system. These included schools in the Free School Movement, schools that promoted progressive ideals by emphasising individual child-centered achievement and fulfilment, and Freedom Schools that were designed to offer high quality educational opportunities to children who were being poorly served by existing public schools, namely minority students.

The schools, which failed to survive over time, shifted in the types of alternative education options available to students. Many alternative schools today are more likely to be viewed by public education systems as disciplinary and/or remedial in nature. Yet, as alternative education programmes have evolved and matured, they have provided lessons not only about how to reconnect with disenfranchised youth, but also how regular schools can avoid disconnection in the first place.

Most of the reforms currently pursued in traditional schools are practices that alternative schools pioneered. The fact that regular school systems often still consider alternative schools as disciplinary even as some alternative education approaches have been incorporated into some regular schools is important to bear in mind as future policy and practice decisions about expanding high-quality options for disconnected youth are made.

13.2. Strategies of Teaching

In alternative education, students find spare time for fulfilling their educational objectives. So, the teaching strategies, beliefs and support services facilitate growth in academic, personal/social and career development initiatives. Often states and communities have statutory requirements governing the numbers of students an alternative education programme or school can have, the type of curriculum that can be used, who can teach the programme, the length of the school day, attendance policies, participation in state-wide student achievement tests, and other similar issues.

Alternative education programmes and schools are defined and designed along a variety of often overlapping dimensions including who is served, where it operates, what the programme offers, and how it is structured or administered.

13.2.1. Target Audience

Socio-economic factors are the main hindrance for attaining education. Many alternative education programmes target specific groups of youth, particularly those considered "at-risk." The targeting is generally what makes such programmes alternative, and the circumstances or needs of the targeted group are what drive the curriculum or approach. These target groups are:

- Women/girls
- Pregnant/parenting teens
- Suspended/expelled students
- Recovered drop-outs
- Delinquent teens
- Low-achievers, and
- All at-risk youth

13.2.2. Location

The location has an important part in conducting alternative education. It should be easily accessible for the students. Alternative education programmes can be physically and administratively located in many different places, and sometimes the location is what makes the programme "alternative."

Two related operational aspects that describe alternative education programmes are first, how the alternative programme relates to regular education, and second, where the programming actually occurs.

The operational setting, or location, where the actual alternative education takes place is somewhat related to the programme's connection to a regular school, but there is variation. Separate alternative education programmes not under the sponsorship of a school are more likely to be located separately, but some programmes have arrangements to operate in school buildings.

The locations of a few alternative programmes are:

— Regular schools during school hours
— School buildings during non-school hours
— Community or recreation centers
— Former school buildings
— Juvenile justice corrections or detention centers
— Store-front neighbourhood organisations
— Public housing projects
— Homeless shelters (emergency and transitional)
— Medical or mental health facilities
— Community college or other post-secondary campuses

13.2.3 Objectives

People discontinue their education due to many reasons. Alternative education programmes help them to continue it. But while continuing the education, which was disconnected before, they prefer to achieve certain goals. Instead of taking degrees, they prefer to attain certain professional capabilities. So, alternative education differs from traditional education in what types of credentials, services, and programming they provide, and how. Many different types of credentials may be offered, including:

— Regular high school diplomas
— General Educational Development (GED) diplomas, or
— Occupational and skills certification

Depending on the type of credential offered, the content of the programming often varies. But many of them are focused on relaying to their students basic skills. This is because the programmes are often short and there is not enough time to cover significant amounts of theory; many students lack basic skills, so that becomes the primary focus of instruction; and specific skills are often what the students want to learn. In addition to basic life skills, many alternative education programmes emphasise career development or employment preparation and provide students multiple career pathway options, including:

— Career awareness/choices workshops
— Occupational exploration programmes
— Apprenticeships
— Modified work/study programmes
— Speakers' bureau
— Work visitations
— Tech-Prep (technical preparation in partnership with a community college)
— Vocational/technical training
— School to work programmes
— Work experience
— Internships

13.3. Typology

The students of alternative education prefer to select subjects which are directly related to their profession. "What" alternative education programmes do or what they offer has been used as a basis for several classifications developed to date. One commonly cited three-level classification is that developed by Dr. Mary Anne Raywid. Raywid's typology has been described as follows:

13.3.1. Type I Programmes

Type I schools offer full-time, multiyear, education options for students of all kinds, including those needing more individualisation, those seeking an innovative or challenging curriculum, or dropouts wishing to earn their diplomas. A full instructional programme offers students the credits needed for graduation. Students choose to attend.

The other characteristics include divergence from standard school organisation and practices (deregulation, flexibility, autonomy, and teacher and student empowerment); an especially caring, professional staff; small size and small classes; and a personalised, whole-student approach that builds a sense of affiliation and features individual instruction, self-paced work, and career counselling. Models range from schools-within-schools to magnet schools, charter schools, schools without walls, experiential schools, career-focused and job-based schools, dropout recovery programmes, after-hours schools, and schools in atypical settings like shopping malls and museums.

13.3.2. Type II Programmes

Discipline is the distinguishing characteristic of Type II programmes, which aim to segregate, contain, and reform disruptive students. Students typically do not choose to attend, but are sent to the school for specified time periods or until behaviour requirements are met. Since placement is short-term, the curriculum is limited to a few basic, required courses or is entirely supplied by the "home school" as a list of assignments. Familiar models include last-chance schools and in-school suspension.

13.3.3. Type III Programmes

Type III programmes provide short-term but therapeutic settings for students with social and emotional problems that create academic and behavioural barriers to learning. Although Type III programmes target specific populations-offering counselling, access to social services, and academic remediation-students can choose not to participate. Raywid's first group of programmes, thus, includes many of the original types of alternative education for at-risk youth established in the U.S., and these are often referred to as "popular innovations" or "true educational alternatives."

13.4. Changing Needs of Education

By education, we all wish to achieve a good job and a decent life. Education also determines our status in the society a certain level. Education makes people to face all adversities in life. The society is ever changing and is the needs of the society. So, education should be capable to fulfil the needs of the society. An alternative education programme is often defined by the programme's characteristics, such as programmes that focus on behaviour, interest, or functional level. Behavioural programming might be designed for students who need a structured setting to focus on more appropriate school behaviours to facilitate their learning and the learning of others. Programmes designed around student interest might include an environmental programme or vocational academies. Functional-level programmes might include high school completion, academic, or skill remediation.

13.4.1. Educational Needs of Students

The needs of students vary time to time. As society develops, the needs of it also changes. A final promising typology is one that centers on students' educational needs. Rather than focusing on a student's demographic characteristics or programmatic category, this typology focuses on the educational problems or challenges students present. These include programmes for:

— Students face a number of problems during their learning stage. Students who have fallen "off track" simply because they have gotten into trouble and need (short-term) systems of recovery to get them back into high schools. The goal of getting them back into regular high schools is appropriate and realistic for this group.

— Students who are prematurely transitioning to adulthood either because they are about to become parents, or have home situations that do not allow them to attend school regularly (e.g., immigrant children taking care of siblings while their parents work, those coming out of the juvenile justice system with many demands on their time, etc.).

— Criminal track records and pregnancy may prevent many to continue education. Students who are substantially off track educationally, but are older and are returning to obtain the credits they need to transition into community colleges very rapidly.

— There is a group of students who are substantially behind educationally-they have significant problems, very low reading levels, and are often way over age for grade. Many of these children have been retained repeatedly and a number of them have come out of special education services. This is a very large group of kids, and most school systems do not have any programmes that can serve meet their needs.

Programmes targeted at particular demographic group, such as pregnant and parenting teens, could be serving kids with a wide variety of educational needs: those who are two credits away from graduation; those who are wards of child welfare agencies and who have multiple problems such as being far over age for grade, and with only a third and fourth-grade education levels; others who are pregnant and parenting but also involved in the juvenile justice system; and yet others with significant behavioural problems. So a single school or programme is being expected to handle too much educational diversity (one that regular school are unable to handle well), and this may be setting the programmes (and their students) up for educational failure.

13.4.2. Administration

The success of alternative education depends on its administration. Alternative education describes "how" alternative education programmes are administered or funded. The administrative dimension is somewhat related to other features of alternative education, but considering it separately helps clarify another aspect of what makes alternative education programmes "alternative."

Alternative education programmes are sponsored or administered by a variety of entities including:

— Non-profit and community-based organisations (CBOs);

— State or local education agencies;

— Charter schools;

— Adult education divisions or agencies;

— Juvenile justice agencies;
— Public or private schools;
— Health or mental health institutions;
— Federally-funded programmes and contractors.
— Private for-profit companies;

Besides serving different types of students in different locations, many alternative education programmes have different policies and administrative procedures than those typically found in regular schools.

The nature of work also influences alternative education programmes. It means the policies and administration that are more similar to those in the workplace (e.g., work teams, supervisors, time cards, or scheduling academic instruction in conjunction with work or apprenticeships). As in regular education settings, alternative programmes also vary tremendously in their academic standards, structure and accountability mechanisms, basic goals and objectives, parent and community involvement, disciplinary policies, and crisis intervention procedures.

There is no specific literature that relates specifically to administrative accountability in alternative education. There are, though, special issues to consider in this area, mainly because accountability and outcome measures used in mainstream schools are not always appropriate for alternative education. For example, using graduation from high school or completion of a degree is not relevant for an alternative education programme that is mainly transitional in nature (e.g., aims to transition students back into regular schools or out of a special programme such as juvenile detention or a treatment center).

The alternative education accountability measures should include shorter-term measures and measures that track continuous "added value" or recognise that some youth may cycle in and out of a programme before experiencing steady progress. Other performance outcomes might include measures of student motivation, learning to learn, and ability to master content. Presumably, programme administrators and agencies sponsoring alternative education programmes do have some type of internal management information, and it can be expected that as the field continues to develop, more reports and documents will be produced on this topic.

The alternative education programmes cannot run smoothly without adequate funds. Funding structures among alternative education programmes are also highly variable. Most alternative education programmes' budgets are based on a variety of unreliable funding sources, such as grants, charitable contributions, and fees for service. Some alternative education programmes may also receive state and local education funds-although these funds are often less than the per-pupil funding those traditional schools receive.

The typology does not map onto any one of these dimensions perfectly. However, a clearer understanding of the many dimensions of alternative education efforts can help in the development of a typology. These dimensions are important to understand for developing a variety of high-quality alternative education options. These options, which meet the needs of all youth who are not being well served by traditional public schools, include programmes and schools that serve children with different needs/characteristics (who), are located in different places (where), provide different types of certificates, diplomas, and programming (what), and are structured, administered, and funded in different ways according to the best needs and interests of students and the community (how).

13.5. Features of Promising Programme

The effectiveness of alternative education programmes can link specific programme characteristics with specific student outcomes. As with other fields of inquiry in their early stages, much of the literature on alternative education presents features or characteristics thought to be essential to the success of alternative education efforts.

13.5.1. High Academic Standards/Expectations

Alternative education aims to achieve high academic standards. Successful programmes/schools set clear and high education standards and expectations for their students. The curriculum in these programmes is not diluted or "watered down." Furthermore, the curricula are often expanded to enhance the educational and vocational interests of the students.

13.5.2. High Standards for Interpersonal/Social Interactions

Education helps people to develop their interactive skills. Successful alternative education programmes/schools have well defined standards of behaviours. And in addition to having strict and clear expectations that are consistently applied to everyone, successful alternative programmes/schools rely on interventions and expanded curricula that foster the development of interpersonal and social skills. Most address issues such as family life, peer pressure, and conflict resolution.

13.5.3. Student-Centered Education and Intervention Plans

The main objective of alternative education programme is to develop the abilities of the students. Successful programmes/schools have their structure, curricula, and support services designed with both the educational and social needs of the students in mind. Therefore, it is imperative that alternative programmes/schools provide the assessment and support services needed to clearly identify and address the cognitive, emotional, health and socio-economic factors affecting the education and development of participating students.

13.5.4. Teacher/Student Ratio

Each and every student needs specific attention to develop their skills. If the number of students in a class is higher, the individual attention from the part of teachers will be less. So, low teacher/student ratios are important to the success of alternative education efforts. Ranging from 8-25 students per teacher, successful efforts have an average ratio of 1-16.

13.5.5. Site-Based Management/Flexibility

While having clear and strong accountability measurements and systems, successful alternative programmes and schools are often free from centralised management. Administrators, teachers, support services staff, students, and parents are involved in the different aspects of the programmes/schools that they participate in.

13.5.6. Parent and Community Involvement

Parents and community have an important role to educate the

school drop outs and its involvement is critical for the success of alternative programmes/schools. All of the programmes and schools identified in various research projects noted that the parents of prospective students must agree to participate in clearly defined ways beyond parent-teacher meetings. Some require that parents volunteer some of their time to the programme/school, others that they participate in family life seminars.

13.5.7. Programme Vs School

The alternative education should be based on either programmes or schools. Programmes are intended for students who may need short term interventions to get through a particular problem or situation that is having a negative impact on their education. They are designed with the goal of helping the student get back in the "regular" school setting as soon the presenting problem or situation is addressed and corrected. On the other hand, schools are designed for students that for one reason or another are better off obtaining an education outside the traditional school setting. Often, these schools include students who must work to help support themselves and their families, or students who need specialised services and interventions but who can meet high education standards.

13.5.8. Location

The success of alternative education programme or school also depends on the location. Programmes are often set within a traditional school. At times they are located within a community school or agency. On the other hand, most alternative schools have their own facilities, share a facility with a larger school, or are located within community colleges or a university campus. Regardless of the location, successful programmes and schools provide healthy physical environments that foster education, emotional well-being, a sense of pride, and safety.

13.5.8.1. Clear focus on academic learning

The alternative education programmes should be focused cleared for implementing it effectively. The most promising schools have a clear focus on academic learning that combines high academic standards with engaging and creative instruction.

13.5.8.2. Ambitious professional development

Teachers are the biggest source of information for the students. So teachers must be very talented and they should be ready to upgrade with latest happenings. Successful schools provide teachers with stimulating, ongoing professional development activities that help teachers to maintain an academic focus, enhance teaching strategies, and develop alternative instructional methods.

Properly designed staff development involves teacher input, work with colleagues, and opportunities to visit and observe teaching in other settings. When given opportunities to examine differences between instructional aspirations and actual practice, teachers will achieve what they aspire to do, provided that they have adequate staff development and support.

13.5.8.3. Decision-making

This is a major player in determining the success of alternative education programmes. Effective service delivery requires decision making at the service delivery level. Decisions about staffing, leadership, budgets, scheduling, curriculum, and pedagogy need to be made by teaching and support staff who have direct contact with students. Effective schools provide autonomy that builds trust and loyalty among staff. Further, giving staff a voice in decision making promotes creativity and instructional excellence.

13.4.8.4 Sense of community

Mostly schools focus on the creation and maintenance of communities. Such intentional communities are more likely to succeed than bureaucratically organised schools. Within effective school communities, students and staff share expectations for learning, and students are encouraged to take a variety of courses and activities that enable them to pursue their interests and aspirations.

13.5.9. Home-School Communication

High academic standards and expectations are the key features of successful programmes. Other important qualities are small schools and class sizes, and high-quality student-centered programmes that actively engage teachers, parents, and other community members. Finally many of them point to the importance of administrative and bureaucratic autonomy for the programme or school, so that they can create "intentional communities" often with the requirement that teachers and students be in the programme voluntarily. Many of these key qualities will need to be considered further as interest in alternative education programmes increases over the coming years, and as evaluation strategies are considered to empirical analyse their effectiveness.

13.6. Conclusion

Education has a vital role in the economic and physiological development of a person. A well educated person will think rational for the benefit of him and select a way accordingly to keep him healthy mentally and physically. But in underdeveloped and developing nations, the number of educated people will be less.

Education is the panacea for all evils. So every government must undertake education process effectively and efficiently. The authorities should consider seriously each and every aspect relating to non-formal education for an impeccable execution of this programme.

References

Lange, Cheryl M. and Sletten, Sandra J., "Alternative Education: A Brief History and Research Synthesis", *Project FORUM*, National Association of State Directors of Special Education, Alexandria, VA, February 1, 2002.

Leone, Peter E. and William Drakeford, "Alternative Education: From a "Last Chance" to a Proactive Model," *The Clearinghouse*, Vol. 3, No. 2, The Helen Dwight Reid Educational Foundation, Heldref Publications, Washington, DC, November/December 1999.

Drakeford, "Alternative Education: From a "Last Chance" to a Proactive Model," The *Clearinghouse, Vol.* 3, No. 2, The Helen Dwight Reid Educational Foundation, Heldref Publications, Washington, DC, November/December 1999.

14

Emerging Trends in Adult Education

14.1. Introduction

The development of a nation depends on the educational status of adults. But due to the galloping expenditure on education prevent many from formal education. For them, government is adopting various measures. Adult education is the practice of teaching and educating adults. This often happens in the workplace, through 'extension' or 'continuing education' courses at secondary schools, at a college or university. Other learning places include folk high schools, community colleges, and lifelong learning centers. A difference is made between vocational education, mostly undertaken in workplaces and frequently related to upskilling, and non-formal adult education including learning skills or learning for personal development.

Educating adults differs from educating children in several ways. One of the most important differences is that adults have accumulated knowledge and experience that can add or hinder the learning experience. Because of the self-direction and motivation of adult learners, they manage to adapt and incorporate the components of academia into their complex life. However, this is a challenge for underprepared adult learners. With their desire to participate in academia, also comes the reality of their deficiencies in foundational skills; thus, they require more than just a superficial introduction to programmes and services.

When we become adults, we realise the importance of education in life and we take initiative to attend collages. Such learners are inclined to be self-directed, motivated, and responsible is appropriate. However, this is not necessarily the case for learners who do not possess the skill-sets to overcome the challenges of academia. For underprepared adult learners, although the motivation to improve their circumstances in life is great, the skills required for academic success may be minimal or absent; as a result, they are ill-prepared to accomplish the academic task required in higher education.

Adult education is different from formal education. So, the educators need to focus on the needs, interests, and desires of their adult learners. However, in fulfilling these attributes, educators first have to understand who these adult learners are, how they learn, and why they enter the learning process. Attention to these attributes allows underprepared adult learners to improve their academic potential. The fulfilment of adult students' needs and interests as the fundamental function of institutions.

The curriculum of adult education is focused in the students' needs and interests. Thus, adult education signifies the modern quest for life's meaning. Adults use education as an extenuation of life; therefore, adult education is about learning in adulthood. Its purpose is to put meaning into the whole of life. However, with the graduation of adult learners who are still ill-equipped in reading, writing, and critical thinking skills, it is pertinent to reflect on the work of higher education. Thus, if educational institutions have diluted the concept of learning and scholarship, they have circumvented the intentions of adult educators in their efforts to develop and establish a stellar foundation for the field of adult education.

Many underprepared adult learners enter academia because of their motivation, their need to know, job growth potential, and many other reasons; this indicates that they do possess some andragogical characteristics.

The adults, however, need a great deal of help to direct their own learning effectively. Adult learners are, oftentimes, not viewed as they really are, but as they are expected to be, as determined by the historical literature that supports this field of study. With such expectations, there is a presumption that underprepared adult learners understand their deficiencies and, based on the ideals of self-direction, know how to compensate for the academic skills they require for achieving success.

The adult learning programmes should be developed to substantively address the needs of underprepared learners. Otherwise, it will not benefit the learners. The individuality and the cognitive aptitude of adult learners determine how such learners "fit" into the fundamental assumptions that drive much of the adult learning community.

The adult educator plans and directs the change process as it relates to the individual learner, learner groups, or the institutional learner system. Accordingly, underprepared adult learners should have a fighting chance of harnessing and incorporating the essential components and skills inherent in their learning environment. They are able to do so when the change agent assists learners in evaluating their successes or failures in needs attainment and helps them replan when necessary. However, if adult educators do not harness their roles as change agents, underprepared adult learners will, somehow, move through the academic system without experiencing "genuine" education; as defined by the movement, growth, and thinking that results from the educational experience.

14.2. Means of Existence

The lives of adults have been entrenched in venues that are worlds apart from academia. So, a proportionate number of underprepared adult learners are not familiar with the nature and expectations of higher education. Therefore, the motivation of these learners to rise above their life circumstances is admirable and laudable, but this does not eliminate the deficiencies with which they enter academia.

When the adults enter into learning, they face a lot of challenges. These deficiencies position them to continue facing academic challenges that would be fewer, if they were better prepared for the academic requirements essential for academic success. Some deficiencies are: poor reading and writing, ineffective communication skills, and also poor to marginal analytical and critical thinking skills. Nonetheless, the only option for improving their "lot" in life is to venture through the gates of higher education.

The adult learners also face some pressures and experiences in their academic life. These pressures, potentially, influence the performance and enhance the struggles of adult learners as they participate in academia because they are usually pressed for time and often have more than one job, in addition to a home and family. Moreover, they may face family disagreements that can shake their world and increase their chaos as well as the need to overcome the cataclysmic effect of divorce that often stretches them to their limits, as they address money and time constraints. This adds perspective to the mind-set of this learner population.

The adult educators try to address certain components which are related to adult learners such as (a) transmitting information via lectures, (b) demonstrating new skills, (c) assisting the learner in planning learning activities, (d) facilitating a discovery learning process, (e) directing the learner to other resources, (f) leading the learner through a series of trial-and-error experiences as well as adhering to institutional fit and supplying the student service needs of adult learners. It becomes the primary responsibility of learners to determine how to achieve academic success.

It is imperative that institutions recognise the type of adult learners they attract, and map out a sound academic path for accepting learners who are not equipped with foundational academic skills. Evidently, the type of college environment makes a difference in what underprepared adult learners retain from their college experience.

14.3. Qualities of Institutions

For the successful implementation of adult learning process, the institutions must posses certain qualities. Many colleges/universities are grappling with the quality of adult learners who enter their doors; however, because of enrolment and retention concerns, many underprepared adult learners are admitted under the belief that they can be successful. Unfortunately, success is only attainable if academia address the true deficiencies of this population and not presume underprepared adult learners have the wherewithal and skill-sets to do so themselves.

First of all, the institution must be efficient enough to carry out the degree programme to the adult learners. If such a concept is not integrated into the enrolment procedures, it becomes the problem of professors to deal with learners who have no chance of succeeding in a chosen course. To maintain institutional standards and enrol the right calibre of learners, it is best that educational institutions acknowledge the limitations of underprepared adult learners and implement appropriate measures to enhance their basic skills; thus, the learning environment created will be beneficial to supporting such learners throughout the academic process.

The atmosphere of the institution must be favourable to maintain the quality of adult learners. Adult educators should have an understanding of adult learners; provide a climate conducive to learning; provide a contextual setting for the exploration of ideas, skills, and resolutions; provide a forum for critical reflection; and have the ability to assist adults in the process of learning how to change our perspectives, shift our paradigms, and replacing one way of interpreting the world by another.

Adult learners can be potentially successful at this level of education. If not, institutions should have a strong system of counselling out adult learners when it is foreseen that such learners do not have the necessary acumen to traverse the challenges of academia. It is a humane act because it benefits the learner in not spending precious dollars in a programme that will not lead to programme completion, and it benefits the institution because the academic standards remain intact.

The institutions must provide a relaxed, trusting, mutually respectful, informal, warm, collaborative, and supporting learning environment. However, such andragogical methods, unaided, do not ensure academic adeptness of underprepared adult learners. If these adult learners are prepared to further themselves, enhance their skills, and improve upon their academic prowess, it will be influenced by what they acquired from the learning environment in tandem with how they implement the learned skills; therefore, more intricate, hands-on and specifically designed programmes, are imperative for underprepared adult learners.

14.3.1. Factory of Excellence

The social climate no longer offers great possibilities for adults without a college education, there is a great upsurge, over the past years, of adults returning or entering higher education. The adult learners, who discontinue education after two or four years with deficient writing and critical thinking skills, need a resurgence because the common thread among these underprepared adults learners, irrespective of their academic aptitude, is their ability to take their business somewhere else, if they are unable to strengthen their marginal skills. Thus, recruitment and retention continue to be familiar bedfellows. As such, it is incumbent upon colleges to facilitate academic pathways that are supportive of underprepared learners as they strive to improve academic skills as well as college survival skills, in their preparation to attempt the challenges of mainstream courses.

The processes presently in place are failing many learners. Two and four year institutions must place more emphasis on establishing programmes that inform and better prepare underprepared learners for their academic experience. Although programmes in the form of orientation, various academic skills improvement seminars/workshops and counselling exist, there is still a significant gap in the intentions of such support programmes and what actually occur; therefore, the diminished skills of such learners are continually perpetuated.

14.3.2. Multicultural Immersion Programme (MIP)

The Multicultural Immersion Programme teaches the concepts of multicultural awareness, understanding, and sensitivity using the urban community as its primary educational resource. This innovative, culturally relevant, community-based multicultural model of adult education was created by a diverse group of concerned community members to address the racial tension this city often experiences. The design, mission, and goal of this programme contribute to our understanding of multicultural immersion programming and identify several processes that would be useful in replicating this type of programming in a variety of settings where adults learn.

Racial tension, unemployment, and poverty are social evils. A community-based multicultural education centered programme can curtail such problems in a certain level.

14.3.2.1. Community-based education

Education is the yardstick of a person's ethos. We learn good behaviours from schools and colleges. So, through community based education, we can eradicate social evils such as abuse, housing, violence, crime, teen pregnancy, ill literacy, and various kinds of discrimination using a broad range of resources.

14.3.2.1. Responsibility of the community

The community has a great responsibility to uplift the conditions of people. If the people in a community are very educated there will not arise the problem of racial or religious discrimination or any clashes. So, the city and county government, the clergy, and civil rights and community organisations are the responsibility to maintain peace among people.

14.4. Experiential Learning

Experiential learning is the process of human cognition achieved by differentiating meaning derived from theoretical and non-formal life experiences with that attained through formal education. Human and societal development depends on learning. However, it is an individual experience. Due to the fact that students bring with them an infinite variety of genetics, predispositions and past experiences, each will leave with a different interpretation of any new learning that takes place. The only true education comes through the stimulation of the individual's powers by the demands of the social situations in which he finds himself.

Education brings a better life to the people. That is why education and experience is tantamount to human development. The formal, curriculum-based education might be cautious in its approach to learning in that most curricula teach, especially in the case of children, knowledge that will not have experiential applications for years to come. Experience is twofold: the active element relating to the actual performance of an action, and the passive element relating to the consequences arising from the active element. Learning from experiences requires the development of a conscious rationalisation both backward and forward in time in relation to an experience.

Experiential learning is education that occurs as a direct participation in the events of life. Learning is informal and is precipitated by people themselves, rather than under the umbrella of a specific institution. Learning is the output of reflecting on everyday experiences. This is the most common way that people learn.

14.4.1. Understanding Experiential Learning

We learn a lot of things from the experiences of our daily life. This is known as experiential learning. It refers to the methodologies attached to non-formal education and the translation of that learning into formal academic credit. On the other hand, it refers more to personal survival and day-to-day decision-making and problem solving.

Life is the biggest institution. Experiential learning may be at a crossroads, opening a new paradigm in education arising from a variety of stimuli that include such factors as cultural and political ideologies, desired and changing levels of empowerment, and social conditions. There appears to be a shift away from the concept of education and towards the concept of learning such that "the value of any experience will depend not so much on the experience of the subject, important though this is, but on the struggles around the way that experience is interpreted and defined and by whom," in attempting to provide a framework for thinking about a field of learning that is in a state of change.

An individual's society and culture play a role in shaping meaning perspectives and meaning schemes. People may be more predisposed to thought and reflection once their basic security needs are met. This line of thinking appears to discount the impacts on learning caused by ideologies other than those deemed to represent free societies. It also contradicts the concept of learning as an individual activity.

Effective learning entails the possession of four different abilities. These are often represented in a quadrant format with observation/reflection and application to new situations at opposing ends of a vertical axis, and formation of concepts/ principles and concrete experience occupying the extremes on the horizontal axis.

Experiential learning steps beyond the bounds of simple cognitive learning. It helps to develop the relationship of the whole learner in the whole of his or her environment, for the whole of his or her life. Learning is the transformation of experience into knowledge, skills, and attitudes.

14.4.2. Association with Learning

Experimental learning has a broad meaning and it can not be refrain in a single definition. It has broad outcomes depending on a variety of circumstances as wide ranging as personal interests, politics, ideologies, and even geography, and one that does not necessarily fit into the standards of scientific method. Definitional problems continue when one tries to disentangle the notion of experiential learning from experiences commonly associated with formal education.

Adult learning places the individual at the centre of the process of making meaning. Learners draw from stored knowledge and new experiences to reflect upon and interpret the meanings associated with learning. This process is an oscillation between new experiences and existing mental constructs with the goal of incorporating the new experiences within the known inventory of constructs.

The psychoanalytic perspective provides approaches to such abstract concepts as the unconscious, the underlying tensions between the learner, knowledge and the educator, and the potential resistance to knowledge. Often these dilemmas arise from a conflict between the conscious and the unconscious in such a way that the unconscious cannot often be educated, but that it has a direct impact on the decisions of the conscious mind. Learning is, in this perspective, the process of toleration exercised with respect to internal conflicts resulting from a fear of fully knowing one's self.

Experience is the good teacher. Adults do not learn from experience, they learn in it. Knowledge forms a critical part of the process of participation in the present, not something to be absorbed, transformed and potentially used in the future. Particularly important to the individual is the community in which they find themselves. If learning occurs through interaction, then it is only through interactions with an immediate community that it occurs. In this case, understanding is achieved through consensus and interaction with others. It is a negotiation between the individual and the community and individuals improve as they develop greater appreciations for the constraints and allowances within which they live.

Power is a central issue in the critical cultural perspective. An understanding of the power structures and hierarchy of dominance in society lead to an understanding of a variety of means for resistance. It is through resistance, according to critical cultural pedagogy, that individuals become open to the unexpected and unimagined. Institutions, such as norms, codes, signs, and categories, form the basis for power determination and, thus, individuals learn "through accepted social discourse to discern blurring borders and categories."

The focus of enactivism is not on the individual experiences or interactions between two components. Rather, it highlights the relationship between the components such that learning is a constant process of understanding relationships.

14.4.3. Need for Evaluation

Individuals became curious about the transferability of credit for their informal learning to their formal education. Getting a grip on some aspects of experiential learning is a lot like trying to catch poplar fluff on a windy day. It is clearly difficult to develop a definition or a learning theory that encompasses all opinions and thoughts on the subject mostly because the field of experiential learning has not made significant empirical progress.

Individuals could progress on the basis of a formal evaluation of a curriculum against demonstrated performance. PLA is, therefore, an attempt to oblige experiential learning to 'conform' to the scientific method. By doing so, a variety of outcomes, such as learner satisfaction, credits awarded, and graduate success, can be scrutinised.

There has been little consideration afforded the means of learning as long as the outcomes desired were achieved. This undermines the value of the learning process. A balance should be found that incorporates both the means and the ends, without harming the independent nature of experiential learning.

14.5. Future Trends in Experiential Learning

The process of experiential learning has shown marked progress over the years but considerable growth is still required. As requirements and challenges become better defined through greater and broader participation and continued research, the best course(s) to follow will undoubtedly emerge.

The practice and progress with and within experiential learning have allowed for the opportunity to debate, discuss and, indeed, reflect upon the field and its implications with respect to learners, learning providers and society as a whole. Further evidence of paradigmatic shift is provided through the growth of importance of prior learning assessments in which formal credits are increasingly being sought for learning achieved through informal and non-formal means in and through an ever-increasing variety of situations and institutions.

Though the future of experiential learning seems secure, a considerable development is also needed. After all, learning is all about the learner. As we progress, taking risks and engaging in new experiences along the way, of course, we increase the opportunities available to ourselves for reflection and redefinition of our meaning perspectives and meaning schemes which will, in turn, motivate us to explore and delve yet further field.

14.6. Conclusion

Ignorance brings a lot of catastrophes in the life of people. Some diseases, cheating, poverty etc are some of such miseries. Adult education and experimental learning help to reduce such kind of unfavourable things. Realising the importance of education, everybody gives priority to adult learning and continuous education. The governments all over the world are also giving priority to educate its masses.

References

Alexander, P. A., Schallert, D. L, & Hare, V. C., "Coming to terms: How researchers in learning and literacy talk about knowledge", *Review of Educational Research*, 1991.

Brah, A., & Hoy, J., "Experiential learning: A new orthodoxy?", In S. Weil & I. McGill (Eds.), *Making sense of experiential learning: Diversity in theory and practice*, Buckingham, UK: Open University Press, 1989.

Brookfield, S. D., *Adult learning, adult education and the community*, Milton Keynes, UK: Open University Press, 1983.

_______________ ., "The concept of critically reflective practice", In A. L. Wilson & E. R. Hayes (Eds.), *Handbook of adult and continuing education*, San Francisco: Jossey Bass, 2000.

Clark, M. C., & Wilson, A. L., "Context and rationality in Mezirow's theory of transformational learning", Adult Education Quarterly, 1991.

Courtney, S., "Defining adult and continuing education", In S. B. Merriam & P. M. Cunningham (Eds.), *Handbook of adult and continuing education,* New York: Jossey-Bass, 1989.

Criticos, C., "Media, praxis and empowerment", In S. Weil & I. McGill (Eds.), *Making sense of experiential learning: Diversity in theory and practice,* Buckingham, UK: Open University Press, 1989.

English, L. M., Boud, D., Fenwick, T. J., Finger, M., Hunt, C., Lander, et al., "Scribes and sorcerers - The production of knowledge and the un/making of an encyclopedia of adult education", *Proceedings of the 45th Annual Adult Education Research Conference,* 2004.

Fenwick, T. J., "Expanding conceptions of experiential learning", *A review of the five contemporary perspectives in cognition,* Adult Education Quarterly, 2000.

Bibliography

Aggarwal, J.C., *Progress of Education in Free India: Modern Indian Education and its problems*, Arya, New Delhi, 1977.

Alexander, P. A., Schallert, D. L, & Hare, V. C., "Coming to terms: How researchers in learning and literacy talk about knowledge", *Review of Educational Research*, 1991.

Aspin, D., Chapman, J., Hatton, M., and Sawano, Y. (eds.), *International Handbook of Lifelong Learning*, London: Kluwer, 2001.

Baden, C. (Ed.), *New Directions for Continuing Education: Competitive Strategies for Continuing Education*, No. 35. San Francisco: Jossey-Bass, 1987.

Barnahas, A.P., *Caste in Chanding India: The Indian Institute of Public Administration*, New Delhi, 1965.

Basu, A.N., *Education in Modern India*, Orient Book Co., Calcutta, 1947.

Beder, H. (Ed.), *New Directions for Continuing Education: Marketing Continuing Education*, No. 31. San Francisco: Jossey-Bass, 1986.

Bennett, D., "The evaluation of environmental education learning", UNESCO in *Trends in Environmental Education*, 1977.

Brah, A., & Hoy, J., "Experiential learning: A new orthodoxy?", In S. Weil & I. McGill (Eds.), *Making sense of experiential learning: Diversity in theory and practice*, Buckingham, UK: Open University Press, 1989.

Brockett R.G, Hiemstra R., *Self-direction in Adult Learning: Perspectives on Theory, Research, and Practice*, Routledge, New York, 1991.

Brookfield, S. D., *Adult learning, adult education and the community*, Milton Keynes, UK: Open University Press, 1983.

Candy P.C., *Self-direction for Lifelong Learning: A Comprehensive Guide to Theory and Practice*, Jossey-Bass, San Francisco, 1990.

Caron, G and Carr-Hill, R.A., *Non-formal education: information and planning issues*, International Institute for Educational Planning, Paris, 1991.

Carr-Hill, R.A., "Participatory planning in education: testing some concepts", Paris, *UNESCO*, Division of Education Policy and Planning (S15), 1982.

Cassara B (ed.), *Adult Education in a Multicultural Society*, Routledge, New York, 1990.

Cervero, R., *Effective Continuing Education for Professionals*, San Francisco: Jossey-Bass, 1988.

Cervero, R.M., and Scanlan, C.L. (Eds.), *New Directions for Continuing Education: Problems and Prospects in Continuing Professional Education*, No. 27. San Francisco: Jossey-Bass, 1985.

Clark, M. C., & Wilson, A. L., "Context and rationality in Mezirow's theory of transformational learning", Adult Education Quarterly, 1991.

Collins M., "Self-directed learning or an emancipatory practice of adult education: Re-thinking the role of the adult educator", *Proceedings of the 29th Annual Adult Education Research Conference*, Faculty of Continuing Education, University of Calgary, 1988.

Coombs P.H, R.C. Prosser and H. Ahmed, *New paths to learning for rural children and youth*, New York, ICED, 1973.

Coombs, Prosser, R.C and Ahmed, H., *New Paths to learning for rural children and youth*, ICED, New York, 1973.

Courtney, S., "Defining adult and continuing education", In S. B. Merriam & P. M. Cunningham (Eds.), *Handbook of adult and continuing education*, New York: Jossey-Bass, 1989.

Cowan, M., Denzer, S., Deutsch, D, Dos Santos, A, Lambeth, E, Norton, C, Shackleford, J, Stapp, W, Vincent, L, Wilson, T, Yandala, D, Zimbelman K., "The handling of controversy and problem solving in environmental education", *Environmental Education and Information*, Vol. 3. No. 4, 1985.

Criticos, C., "Media, praxis and empowerment", In S. Weil & I. McGill (Eds.), *Making sense of experiential learning: Diversity in theory and practice*, Buckingham, UK: Open University Press, 1989.

Dayal, Bhagwan, *The Development of Modern Indian Education*, Orient Longman, Bombay, 1955.

Dodds, T., "The use of distance in non-formal education", The Commonwealth of Learning and the International Extension College, Cambridge, 1996.

Drakeford, "Alternative Education: From a "Last Chance" to a Proactive Model," The *Clearinghouse, Vol.* 3, No. 2, The Helen Dwight Reid Educational Foundation, Heldref Publications, Washington, DC, November/December 1999.

Edger Faure, et al., "Learning to Be, A World of Education Today and Tomorrow", *UNESCO*, Paris, 1972.

Ekpenyong L E., "Studying adult learning through the history of knowledge", *International Journal of Lifelong Education*, 1990.

Emellin, L., "Environmental Education programme for Adults", In *Trends in Environmental Education*, UNESCO, 1977.

English, L. M., Boud, D., Fenwick, T. J., Finger, M., Hunt, C., Lander, et al., "Scribes and sorcerers - The production of knowledge and the un/making of an encyclopedia of adult education", *Proceedings of the 45th Annual Adult Education Research Conference*, 2004.

Fenwick, T. J., "Expanding conceptions of experiential learning", *A review of the five contemporary perspectives in cognition*, Adult Education Quarterly, 2000.

Field, J. and Leicester, M., *Lifelong Education*, London: Routledge, 2000.

Final report: Intergovernmental Conference on Environmental Education, Paris, France, 1978.

Galanter Marc, *Competing Equalities: Law and the Backward Classes in India*, Oxford, New Delhi, 1984.

Gore, M.S., *Indian Education: Structure and Process*, Rawat Publication, Jaipur, 1995.

Gosal, G. S., "Literacy in India: An Interpretative Study", *Rural Sociology*, 1964.

Gregg, S., "Creating effective alternatives for disruptive students", *Clearing House*, 1999.

Guerin, G. & Denti, L., "Alternative education support for youth at-risk", *Clearing House*, 1999.

Hammond M, Collins R., *Self-directed learning: Critical Practice*, Kogan Page, London, 1991.

Hayes, C. D., *Lifelong learning the search for meaning in a postmodern world*, Wasilla, AK: Autodidactic Press, 1998.

Hesburgh, T. M., Miller, P. A., & Wharton, C. R., *Patterns for lifelong learning*, San Francisco: Jossey-Bass, 1973.

Jolly, K.G., *Literacy for All by 2001: Strategies at District Level*, D.K. Publishers, New Delhi, 1992.

Knox, Alan, *Adult Development and Learning*, San Francisco: Jossey-Bass, 1977.

Kolb, D., *Learning Style Inventory*, McBer & Co., 1976.

La Belle, T.J., "Formal, non-formal and informal education: holistic perspectives on lifelong teaming". In: *International Review of Education*, 1982.

Lange, C.M., "Characteristics of alternative schools and programs serving at-risk students", *High School Journal*, 1998.

Limaye, P.M., *Education in India Today*, Deccan Education Society, Poona, 1945.

Lones, Paul S., "Learning as Creativity: Implications for Adult Learners", *Adult Learning*, 2000.

Merriam, S. B., & Brockett, R. G., *The profession and practice of adult education: An introduction*, San Francisco: Jossey-Bass, 1997.

Merriam, S.B., *An Update on Adult Learning Theory*, New York: Greenwood Press, 1993.

Mezei, K., *Principles of Adult Learning*, Humber College Ed., Toronto, 1991.

Mocker, D. W. and Spear, G. E., *Lifelong Learning: formal, nonformal, informal and self-directed*, Columbus, Ohio: ERIC, 1982.

Moemeka, A.A., "Radio's role in non-formal education", *Prospects vol. 13*, part 4., 1983.

Naik, J.P., *Elementary Education in India: A Promise to keep*, Allied Publishers, Bombay, 1975.

O'riordan, T., *Environmentalism*, Pion Press, 1978.

Oyasi, H., "International and regional co-operation in environmental education", In *Trends in Environmental Education*, UNESCO, 1977.

Panicker, P. N., "KANFED - a private organization promoting adult education", Adult Education and Development, no. 15, 1980.

Pirages, D, and Ehrlich, P., *Arkill : Social response to Environmental Imperatives*, San Francisco W.H. Freeman Press, 1974.

Reghu, V., "Preparation of books for neo-literates in post-literacy and continuing education programmes (India)", Adult Education and Development, 1999.

Renner P., "The Art of Teaching Adults: How to become an exceptional instructor and facilitator", Training Associates, Vancouver, BC, Canada, 1999.

Rutherford, R.B., Jr. & Quinn, M.M., "Special education in alternative education programs", *Clearing House*, 1999.

Sharma Amita, Gopal Krishnan R., *A New Strategy for the Total Literacy Campaign*, Document 5, Rajiv Gandhi Mission, June 1999.

Stapp, WB, Cox, D.A., *Environmental Education Activities Manual*, Thomson-Shore, Dexter, Michigan, U.S.A, UNESCO, 1981.

Tharakan, P K Michael, "Ernakulam re-visited: a study of literacy in the first totally literate District in India", in M. Karlekar (ed), *Reading the World: Understanding the literacy campaigns in India*, Bombay: Asia South Pacific Bureau of Adult Education, 2000.

Index